THE CRUISES OF
GUSTAVUS CONYNGHAM

KENNIKAT AMERICAN BICENTENNIAL SERIES
Under the General Editorial Supervision of
Dr. Ralph Adams Brown
Professor of History, State University of New York

Gustavus Conyngham

LETTERS AND PAPERS
RELATING TO THE CRUISES OF
GUSTAVUS CONYNGHAM
A CAPTAIN OF
THE CONTINENTAL NAVY
1777–1779

EDITED BY
ROBERT WILDEN NEESER

KENNIKAT PRESS
Port Washington, N. Y./London

LETTERS AND PAPERS RELATING TO
THE CRUISES OF GUSTAVUS CONYNGHAM

First published in 1915
Reissued in 1970 by Kennikat Press
Library of Congress Catalog Card No: 76-120887
ISBN 0-8046-1280-3

Manufactured by Taylor Publishing Company   Dallas, Texas

KENNIKAT AMERICAN BICENTENNIAL SERIES

CONTENTS

CONTENTS

CONTENTS

CONTENTS

[xii]

CONTENTS

CONTENTS

[xiv]

CONTENTS

CONTENTS

CONTENTS

ILLUSTRATIONS

INTRODUCTION

"I SEE by your newspapers," wrote Benjamin Franklin to David Hartley[1] during the summer of 1779, "that Capt. Cunningham, one of our cruisers, is at length taken and carried prisoner into England, where it is proposed to try him as a pirate, on the pretence that he had no commission. As I am well acquainted with the fact, I can assure you that he really had a Congress commission. And I cannot believe that mere resentment, occasioned by this uncommon success, will attempt to sacrifice a brave man, who has always behaved as a generous enemy,—witness his treatment of his prisoners taken in the Harwich packet, and all afterwards that fell into his hands."[2]

This was, of course, none other than the famous Captain Gustavus Conyngham, who, in the years 1777 and 1778, so terrorized British commerce by his cruises in the Channel, that London insurance rose to twenty-eight per cent., "higher than at any time in the last war with France and Spain."[3] The name "pirate" was applied to him, as it was to John Paul Jones, by every Englishman of the day, so that it is not surprising to find him referred to in such terms also by George III, in his correspondence with his ministers. But the charge of

[1] A member of Parliament with whom Franklin was on very intimate terms.

[2] Printed in Hale's Franklin in France, Vol. I, p. 342.

[3] Wharton's Revolutionary Diplomatic Correspondence, Vol. II, pp. 262, 311.

piracy could not be maintained against him any better than could the charge of treason be sustained against all American sailors taken in arms against the mother country. That Conyngham had a commission on his first cruise was always believed by some. But the fact was never satisfactorily substantiated during the captain's lifetime, and the brave man died without obtaining the satisfaction of a proper recognition of his services by his own countrymen.

A few years ago there appeared in a catalogue of Charavay, an autograph- and print-seller in Paris, among a score of other notices, the following:

> "143 Hancock (John), célèbre homme d'État Américain, gouverneur du Massachusetts, signataire de la Déclaration de l'Indépendance— Pièce sig. comme président du congrès; Baltimore, 1 mars 1777, 1 p. in-fol. Obl. Rare."

The connection of the names and dates, of course, would, at the outset, attract the attention of any collector of Americana; for, more than likely, they would have something to do with Franklin's sojourn at the Court of France. The price asked was much less than the principal signature alone generally brought in the autograph market, so it was included in a list of small purchases ordered from the catalogue by Captain John S. Barnes, this Society's first president, some years before his lamented death.

When the paper numbered 143 was opened, it was found to be a commission giving the rank of captain in the navy of the United Colonies to one Gustavus Conyngham, and appointing him to the command of the armed vessel Surprize. That was all. But—Gustavus Conyngham! The Surprize! It seemed almost incredible that it could be true!

Yes; it was actually the long missing paper that is mentioned by every historian who has written the history of our Revolutionary navy! There was no doubt of the authenticity of the document; the well known signatures of John Hancock and Charles Thompson were substantiated without difficulty, and, besides, the names written in the blank spaces were found to be in the handwriting of no less a personage than Benjamin Franklin himself!

Here was the document that authorized the sailing from the French port of Dunkirk of the little vessel that flew the red-and-blue-barred rattlesnake flag of the United Colonies! Here was the instrument that is supposed to have saved a score of lives held forfeit to the British crown! Here was the missing evidence, for the lack of which a great case in law was lost and a brave man's heart was broken.

After one hundred and twenty-three years we have at last the lost commission—that document around which was woven a chapter, both recorded and unrecorded, of American history; a drama smacking of romance, filled with mysterious plotting and secret international diplomacy; a strange story of adventure, of war, of tragedy!

To secure a complete collection of papers and documents bearing on the foreign cruises of Gustavus Conyngham, it was necessary to search among both original and printed sources. The most important selection of letters was found in the Stevens "Facsimiles of Manuscripts in European Archives Relating to America,

1773–1783," and in Wharton's "Revolutionary Diplomatic Correspondence." In the "Silas Deane Papers," printed for the New York Historical Society, further important letters were secured, while additional material was obtained from the "Pennsylvania Magazine of History and Geography" and from the contemporary volumes of the London "Remembrancer" and "Chronicle."

But, while this official correspondence has served to form the historic frame in which this remarkable story is set, other papers, fortunately, came to light at the time of the discovery of the lost commission, which offered material such as this Society primarily exists to deal with. For, intimate as the public documents here collected are, these new manuscripts go even deeper into the well-springs of history. This collection comprises the original commission issued to Conyngham by Benjamin Franklin on March 1, 1777, the manuscript journal kept by the captain during his imprisonment in England in 1779, letters from the various American agents in Europe and in the West Indies, lists of prizes captured by the Surprize and Revenge, and other papers bearing on the cruises of these two small vessels.

WHEN the American Revolution broke out, the French Government was careful to adopt a policy in accord with the true interests of their own country, and consistent with the letter, if not with the spirit, of their obligations towards the Government of England. It is true that the Comte de Vergennes pronounced Lord North's attempt to subjugate the colonies by force as "an undertaking against Nature"; but Louis XVI's other advisers were very careful not to show their true hand prematurely lest England and her American colonists should happen to make up their family quarrel and celebrate their reconciliation by joining together in an attack upon the French possessions in the West Indies. So France allowed the civil war to run its course beyond the Atlantic, and patiently awaited the golden opportunity while England tore herself to pieces with her own hands.

It was essential, wrote Vergennes, on March 12, 1776, to persuade George III that the intention of the two Bourbon powers towards England were not only pacific, but positively friendly, in order that the British ministry might be emboldened to entangle themselves, too deep for retreat, in a fierce, dubious, and most exhausting war against their own colonies. The courage of the colonists, on the other hand, would have to be "sustained by secret favours" from France. They should be supplied furtively, but generously, with arms and money, and informed that, while it was below the dignity of the French King to treat openly with insurgents, his Majesty was disposed to recognize them as allies if they ventured upon the decisive step of renouncing their allegiance to the English crown and declaring themselves an independent nation.[1]

But these "Considerations on the Policy" communicated by the Foreign Secretary were intensely distasteful to the King. Louis XVI had no inclination to pose as the tutelary genius of a rebellion. He shrank from entering upon a course of treachery which could not fail to involve his country in a hazardous and protracted conflict. His conviction of duty and his sense of honor

---

[1] Doniol's History, Vol. I, pp. 272–286.

were too great. Besides, "an English war," Turgot warned him, "should be shunned as the greatest of all misfortunes; since it would render impossible, perhaps for ever, a reform absolutely necessary to the prosperity of the State and the solace of the people." But, as the King so often was wont to remark, "except for myself and Turgot, there is no one who really loves the people." Actuated by this unfeigned solicitude for the people committed to his charge, he shrank from wantonly inaugurating, after an interval of only twelve years, another carnival of bloodshed, of national peril, and of private bereavement, impoverishment and ruin. But, with the fall of Turgot, he stood alone against the opinion of his united Cabinet. All his plans for the better government of France, and for the amelioration of the hard lot of her unhappy peasantry, seemed to have been in vain. He felt himself powerless to avert the projected war with England, which shocked his conscience,—a war which, in its consequences, he feared would prove fatal to his reign.

Such was the situation in France when Silas Deane, the first commissioner sent by the American Continental Congress, arrived in Paris in June, 1776. The prospects of cordial relations between the young Republic and the Court of Versailles were most encouraging. Yet nothing but failure seemed destined to follow the diplomatic methods employed by the colonial leaders. Fortunately, at this moment the ability, the discretion, and the force of character of a single man retrieved the day. Benjamin Franklin was a past master in the art of diplomacy. When he landed Caron de Beaumarchais expressed a friendly uneasiness lest the old man, left to his own guidance "in that cursed country of meddling and gossip," should fall into bad hands, and commit some fatal blunder or indiscretion. But this was sympathy wasted. The Pennsylvania veteran had the craft of age without any of its feebleness, as the statesmen of France and Spain and Holland were destined to learn by unpleasant experience. Whoever was left in the lurch, it never was Benjamin Franklin. "From the very first moment of his arrival in Paris," says Trevelyan, "he set himself deliberately, and most artfully, at work to tempt Louis the Sixteenth's Cabinet deeper and deeper into a policy which was the salvation of America, but which, in the end, brought utter ruin upon the French Monarchy." The influence of the great American commissioner was apparent in every department of the French administration. Certain members of the King's Cabinet, who seemed to count for a great deal more than either his Most Christian Majesty or his frugal Swiss banker,[1] were always as eager to give as Franklin was bold to ask. The American commissioners were soon accommodated with a loan of two million francs, bearing no interest and payable "when the United States were settled in peace and prosperity." Another million came from the Farmers General, in exchange for the privilege of buying twenty thousand hogsheads of tobacco from the warehouses of Virginia and Maryland. Four millions, ten millions, and six millions were afterwards forthcoming in three successive years, until the total sum obtained from France by the solicitations of Franklin amounted to six and twenty millions. How thriftily these great loans were expended on the purchase of military stores for Washing-

[1] Jacques Necker.

ton's armies in the colonies, and on the equipment of American cruisers which preyed upon British commerce in European waters, can easily be surmised.[1]

When the cruiser[2] which conveyed Franklin across the Atlantic had deposited him safely at his destination, she ranged the Channel and the Bay of Biscay. Within a few weeks she made five prizes; and her list of captures reached an enormous figure before she finally met her fate. Captain Wickes found in French harbors a sure refuge from danger, a ready market for his captures, and all the necessary facilities for refitting his vessel. When the English ambassador[3] remonstrated, the Court of Versailles gave him fair words, and ostentatiously prohibited any further breach of neutrality in sham orders which, after a brief show of obedience, were openly and systematically disregarded by the port authorities.[4] (See pp. 47, 54–55.)

If such things could be done within the range of diplomatic surveillance and protest, the American commissioners still felt that such a course caused both "trouble and uneasiness to the Court and must not be too frequently practised."[5] But in spite of their remonstrances, these incidents recurred, and so frequently, that in February, 1777, the British Government felt obliged to order a 70-gun ship to the Gulf of Gascony to intercept American vessels trading in French ports, while

[1] The American Commissioners to the Committee of Secret Correspondence, January 17, 1777. See Wharton's Revolutionary Diplomatic Correspondence, Introduction.

[2] The Reprisal. [3] Lord Stormont.

[4] See Allen's Naval History of the American Revolution, Vol. I, pp. 260–261.

[5] Lacour-Gayet's La Marine Militaire de La France sous le Règne de Louis XVI, pp. 87–88.

the Comte de Grasse, with L'Intrépide, 74, and a frigate, cruised in the same waters to protect foreign vessels pursued by the English which claimed his protection.[1]

About this time Gustavus Conyngham appeared at Dunkirk. He was an Irishman by birth, having been born in the County of Donegal in 1747. In his early youth his father emigrated to the colonies, and there he became an apprentice to Captain Henderson in the Antigua trade, and continued with him as sailor and mate, until, by Captain Henderson's death, he was promoted to the command of the vessel in which he had been serving. Then, in 1773, he married Anne Hockley, the daughter of a Philadelphia merchant, and two years later, in the fall of 1775, he sailed from the Quaker city in the Charming Peggy for Holland to bring out from that country some saltpeter and clothing, and, if possible, also munitions of war to aid the colonies that had already begun the struggle against the mother country. Just after entering the Channel he was captured by a British cruiser, but he rose against the prize crew, recaptured his little craft, and brought her safely in behind Texel Island. But the British representatives complained to the Dutch authorities of the character of the Charming Peggy's cargo; her sailing was prevented, and the return voyage abandoned altogether, although on more than one occasion Conyngham was tempted to take advantage of the thick weather and slip out into the Channel. But his ship was a slow sailer and would have had little chance with the swift English cutters that were on guard outside. So Gustavus Conyngham,

[1] Wharton's Revolutionary Diplomatic Correspondence, Vol. II, p. 287.

like many a Yankee shipmate, found himself stranded in Europe, on the lookout for anything to fill up his spare moments and burning to do something (see p. 9).

Through a friend of his named Ross, Conyngham met William Hodge, a Philadelphia merchant in the employ of the American commissioners, who was purchasing vessels at Dunkirk for the Continental naval service, and the latter seems to have recommended the captain to his superiors as a desirable commander for one of these craft. Benjamin Franklin accordingly filled out for him one of the blank commissions which he had received for that purpose, signed by the President of Congress, and dated it March 1, 1777. With this authority, Conyngham returned to Dunkirk, where Hodge had, on April 17, purchased a lugger[1] of English construction, which was renamed the Surprize (see pp. 1, 15, 21, 31, 37, 96, 140, 143, 145).

On May 1, 1777, the Surprize sailed from Dunkirk under the guise of a bona-fide smuggler. But once clear of the roads, she threw off the mask, hoisted the Continental colors, and began to cruise off the mouth of the Meuse. Skilfully eluding the British cruisers on watch before the harbor entrance, Conyngham headed his vessel along the coast of Holland, and within a few days he made his first captures. On May 3 the packet Prince of Orange, en route from Harwich to Helvoetsluis, was intercepted—the third packet that England had ever lost in these narrow seas—and on the day following the 110-ton brig Joseph, bound from Messina to Hamburg, with a cargo of wine, lemons and oranges, was brought

---

[1] The Admiral Pocock. She was sold by her captain, Robert Murdock, for the price of 500 louis d'or (12,000 livres).

to. With these two important prizes Conyngham made the best of his way back to Dunkirk (see pp. 37, 39, 45).

As he entered the port, two English ketches fouled him intentionally, and the Surprize, in consequence of this mishap, sprang a leak. This necessitated an immediate official investigation, as the French marine ordinances specified that no vessel captured by captains under a foreign commission should remain in port for more than twenty-four hours unless restrained by stress of weather or unless the capture had been made from enemies of France. So in order to run no risk of forfeiture of his two prizes, Conyngham asked for the required formal inspection. This he obtained on May 9, and, with the verbal process, also the desired authority to repair his vessel and the permission to dispose of his prizes.[1]

But, in the meantime, the captain of the Joseph had filed protest with the British consul at Ostend. The news reached Paris by special post on the evening of the 7th of May. The next morning Lord Stormont hurried to Versailles and waited on M. de Maurepas[2] and M. de Vergennes. The French ministers seemed surprised at the news which the ambassador had to communicate, and expressed to him their indignation and regret, for their subordinates had not yet apprised them of what had taken place at Dunkirk. M. de Sartine[3] was directed forthwith to order the arrest of Conyngham and of his crew, and to see to the seizure of the Surprize and the release of the two prizes. These instructions were

---

[1] Mims's American Privateers at Dunkerque. (In Proceedings of the United States Naval Institute, Vol. XXXVI, p. 939.)

[2] The French Prime Minister.

[3] The French Minister of Marine.

promptly complied with, and it was on this occasion that Conyngham's original commission was "taken & sent up to Versailles & not returned" (see pp. 1, 16, 19, 24, 30, 44, 45).

Lord Stormont recorded with satisfaction the success of his application "with regard to the Dunkirk Pirate," which, he wrote to his Government, was "highly displeasing to Franklin and Deane." These assurances were well received in London. George III requested his Prime Minister to mention this "strong proof" of the French ministry's intention "to keep appearances" in his speech before the Houses of Parliament, and Lord North dwelt at length upon this extremely satisfactory attitude of the Bourbon court (see pp. 24, 26).

But in this he was not quite correct. A letter received at the Foreign Office a few days later from one of its spies—Dr. Edward Bancroft, a man who received bribes from both parties, for he was in the employ of Franklin as well—confirmed the fact that "Lord Stormont has the ear of the Comte de Vergennes, but," it added, "Franklin has the Queen on his side, and she will do what he says." And this prophecy was not long in being fulfilled. On May 24th, ten days after Lord Stormont penned his exulting note, we find the American commissioners writing that they had already been given to understand that Conyngham would "through favour be discharged with his Vessel." At all events, just before the arrival of the sloops-of-war that were to convey "the Dunkirk Pirate" and his companions to England for trial, orders were brought post-haste from Paris to release the prisoners, and Conyngham and his men were again allowed to roam at large (see pp. 28, 36, 40, 41, 48, 51).

Once more there arose a state of feverish apprehension in British merchant circles. The packet-boat and the brig Joseph, it was true, had been surrendered upon the demand of their ambassador, but this, as Deane remarked, was only a "temporary triumph." With Conyngham again at liberty, they were left in a state of anxious perplexity, because no one could tell when or where he would strike. His movements were closely watched by British spies and agents, and his whereabouts were constantly communicated across the Channel (see pp. 23, 69). The master of a fishing-smack who had seen Conyngham in the streets of Dunkirk lost no time in apprising the postmaster at Harwich of every detail, and this official in turn wrote to the postmaster-general at London that the American was about to put to sea in a "cutter, which is painted blue and yellow, which was built for the smuggling trade, and reported to be a fast sailer," adding that he "thought proper to give this intelligence, and make no doubt of necessary steps being taken to put a stop to the proceedings of this daring pirate" (see p. 46). All this was, of course, duly communicated to Lord Stormont in Paris and to Andrew Frazer, the British commissioner at Dunkirk, so that the French authorities were obliged to take measures accordingly. In order to avoid the recurrence of similar cases, M. de Sartine commanded his representatives to investigate the rumors current about Conyngham, and to prevent the recurrence of affairs such as the English ambassador was making complaint of, but to make these searches "with due prudence."

There were two cutters fitting out at Dunkirk. One of them appeared to be an ordinary smuggler, but the other, the Greyhound, it was "notorious," was actually preparing to leave port under the American flag (see pp. 23, 28, 36, 40, 42, 47, 48, 50, 58, 112, 140). Lord Stormont hastened to file his protest with M. de Vergennes. But the latter answered that "it had not been found upon examination that the Cutter was armed," in spite of the British ambassador's insistence that "she certainly had guns on board, and that those Guns had been purchased in France." However, the Foreign Minister did "take down in writing the Name of *Hodge*" and that of Conyngham on Lord Stormont's dictation and promised to give the matter his immediate attention (see p. 49). Still there was no interruption in the proceedings at Dunkirk. The fitting out of the two cutters, which were none other than the Surprize and the Revenge,[1] proceeded with expedition. One of them was being laden, so it was said, by William Hodge for Ireland, but with a large cargo of ammunition (see pp. 51, 97). Seventeen sailors were being enrolled at Calais for her. Then came an unexpected order from the Ministry of Marine to buy her for the King's service, "if it were such a good sailer" (see p. 53). It looked for a while as if the departure of the vessels would be prevented, after all. But Hodge cleverly anticipated every objection by disposing of the Revenge to an Englishman named Richard Allen, while the Surprize was sold by an Irishman to Dominique Morel, a widow (see pp. 56, 75). The sale of the latter

[1] Formerly the Greyhound. She was a little larger and swifter than the Surprize, and mounted fourteen carriage- and twenty-two swivel-guns. There were no Frenchmen on board (see p. 69) when she stood out of the harbor about the middle of July, but a number seem to have joined the vessel in the offing when Conyngham did, for, later, as many as 66 out of her crew of 106 were mentioned as being French.

aroused the suspicions of the Admiralty of Dunkirk, but no objection was made to the transfer of ownership in the case of the Revenge; Hodge and Allen were merely required to comply with the usual Admiralty formalities and give bond that the cutter would not carry on privateering or take any Frenchmen aboard (see pp. 59, 69). Then a passport was made out for the destination of Bergen in Norway, and the vessel was allowed to get under way (see pp. 68, 84, 145).

The Revenge was no sooner beyond the harbor entrance, on July 17th, than Conyngham took command, under a new commission, "as captain and commander of the armed vessel or cutter called the Revenge," dated May 2, 1777, which the commissioners had purposely dated anterior to the seizure of the old one (see pp. 2, 77). His sailing orders directed him to proceed immediately to America as bearer of despatches, without molesting British shipping unless he was attacked; but verbal instructions which he received on July 15th from William Carmichael, the commissioners' secretary, which "could not be committed to paper," apparently directed him to do exactly the contrary (see pp. 2, 64).

Several transports carrying Hessian troops to England for service in America were known to be in the German Ocean at this moment. But the delays which attended the departure of the Revenge from Dunkirk prevented her from arriving off the mouth of the Thames in time to intercept them. Conyngham thereby "lost a glorious opportunity" (see p. 3). Good fortune, however, pursued the Revenge in another quarter. From the very moment she slipped out under the guns of the hostile men-of-war in the offing, she began to make prizes. On July 21st she captured a large schooner, the Happy Return. Two days later she brought to the brig Maria. Both these vessels and the brig Patty, which was taken in the German Ocean on July 25th, Conyngham would gladly have sent into port in order to realize some prize-money from their sale. But, unfortunately, on each occasion the Revenge found herself in the presence of British ships-of-war and sorely pressed. So there was no alternative but to burn the prizes, except in the case of the Patty, which there was time to ransom for £630 sterling.

Such successes within sight of the very shores of England caused great excitement in London. It was so unexpected, so bold, so audacious. Insurance rose quickly. British ships were no longer considered safe, even in the English Channel. At one time there were as many as forty French vessels loading with English merchandise in the Thames, while it is said that as much as ten per cent. was sometimes paid as insurance for the short passage between Dover and Calais. "In a word," wrote Silas Deane to Robert Morris, "Cunningham, by his first and second bold expeditions, is become the terror of all the eastern coast of England & Scotland, and is more dreaded than Thurot[1] was in the late war" (see p. 98).

"But," concluded Deane, "though this distresses our enemies, it embarrasses us." With the fourth prize the clouds began to gather. On July 26th Conyngham intercepted the brig Northampton, with a rich cargo of hemp and iron. She proved so valuable a prize that it was decided to send her into port. But both prize and prize crew fell into the hands of the British and were taken into Yarmouth roads, where it was discovered that

[1] François Thurot, a famous French corsair of the Seven Years' War.

no less than sixteen out of the twenty-one men manning
the prize were Frenchmen. The British Government
lost no time in communicating these details to their ambassador (see pp. 71, 74, 76–79, 80, 87).

On July 16th Lord Stormont had already been to see
M. de Vergennes about the Revenge, and on that occasion he certainly expressed himself "fully and strongly."
When the "corsair" finally slipped out unmolested, how
he must have wept with rage at having been so easily
duped! After all his representations, "those very Men,
whom M. de Maurepas had formally promised should
be tried as Pirates," were not only set at liberty, but
suffered to put to sea in an armed vessel under the very
eyes of the British commissioner at Dunkirk! It was
true that, in accordance with the French Admiralty re-
quirements, an assurance and bond that the vessel would
not be used as a privateer and would not take any
Frenchmen aboard, were demanded of both buyer and
seller of the Revenge. But what validity had this bond
when the Admiralty took security from Hodge, "who
cannot be considered as a responsible Man in this Case,"
complained Stormont, "and I believe is so in None"?
"Besides Sir," he wrote to Lord Weymouth, "there is
a clear contradiction in this whole affair that appears
upon the face of it, Richard Allen is allowed to declare
the Ship is his Property, and Hodge gives security. If
the Property is not for Hodge how can He answer for
what the crew will or will not do? If he is the owner
how comes Allen to be admitted to make a Declaration
that is manifestly false?" (See pp. 65, 72, 81.)

Then came Lord Weymouth's despatch of the 1st of
August conveying the news of the Revenge's successes
and of the presence of "a considerable number of

French subjects" among her crew (see p. 74). The long-suffering ambassador began to pack up his things and threaten open war, declaring that if a summary example were not made of the American agents, orders would be given to the British cruisers to intercept and seize the French Newfoundland fleet, daily expected from the Grand Banks. In fact, the Court of St. James was already hastening war preparations in England on the suspicion of connivance between the French ministry and the American commissioners. Something had to be done, therefore, to appease Lord Stormont, and done immediately. So the "chef de l'Amirauté" who had allowed Conyngham to escape was "punished by being ordered to attend Court" (see pp. 83, 96), and William Hodge was arrested and confined in the Bastille because "it is a very serious matter to lie to a king, which he hath done."[1] (See pp. 83, 88, 91, 96, 144.) This was on August 11th. A few weeks later the Newfoundland fishing fleet was safely anchored in French ports. Thereupon "Mr. Hodge, an American, detained in the Bastille by the King's orders," was released, and the incident considered closed (see pp. 109, 110, 112).

In the meantime Conyngham continued his successes against English shipping. From the German Ocean he sailed into the region of the Baltic, then back again through the Straits of Dover up to the "Irish Channel & Western Ocean." For two months he kept the sea without seeking a harbor. No stress of weather deterred him. But once, when off the northwest coast of Ireland, the Revenge sprung her bowsprit in a gale, and as the vessel was very short of supplies, Conyngham decided to

[1] Comte de Vergennes to Ferdinand Grand, August 21, 1777.

run into Kinehead for repairs and for "Watter, verry little else to be got theare" (see p. 4).

A little later, the news reached the Continent that a Flemish dogger recently arrived from Iceland had sighted Conyngham at sea about the first week of September. Her captain bore a package of letters and two valises which "the Pirate" had committed into his hands. The Revenge at the time had two prizes in tow and seemed to be making for some French port. Lord Stormont immediately waited on M. de Vergennes with the dogger captain's declaration. The French minister "replied in such a way as to leave no doubt that Cunningham would be punished according to his deserts," and promptly issued orders to arrest him in case he returned to the coasts of France,—though, as he wrote to the Marquis de Noailles in London, "I doubt it, for he could not do a worse thing" (see pp. 99, 100). And Conyngham very likely also feared the consequences, for he kept clear of the French coast, and did not again attempt to make port after leaving the Irish Sea until well in Spanish waters.

One of the Revenge's prizes, the brig Venus, was recaptured, but the others arrived safely at Corunna, Ferrol, and Bilbao, where their interests were well looked after by the commercial houses of Joseph Gardoqui & Sons and Lagoanere & Company (see pp. 100, 106–109). Both these houses had long had business connections in the American colonies, and during the war the latter had firm friends in their Spanish correspondents. In fact, it was their aid and the influence at court of Diego Gardoqui that enabled the Americans to combat the efforts of the British ambassador at Madrid, and contributed so materially to the success of the colonial cause in Spain.[1]

Conyngham, however, made his initial appearance at Bilbao under very unfortunate circumstances. Just before his arrival Lagoanere & Company had cleverly disposed of one of his most valuable prizes, the brig Black Prince, by sending her around to the French port of Bayonne under false papers covering a vessel of Spain, which had been procured from a Spanish merchant in Ferrol. But off Cape Ortegal the Revenge fell in with the French brig Graciosa, having on board dry goods valued at £75,000 sterling, "covered by a Spaniard in Corruna," and fully insured in England,—"thiss and other circumstances," Conyngham wrote, "well known on board revenge." But the crew insisted on making the vessel a prize, and compelled Conyngham to place a crew on board of the Graciosa and order her to Bilbao. This was a flagrant violation of the customs of naval warfare, and the Spanish authorities naturally did not like the proceeding. No sooner had the brig dropped anchor in port than the prize crew were thrown into prison, and it was only with the greatest difficulty and by his submitting to the arbitrary terms of the Spanish governor that Conyngham was able to obtain their release (see pp. 4, 113, 120).

The commissioners in Paris seem to have been kept well advised of the Revenge's movements, for we find Deane writing, in December, that they had received word from Conyngham, under date November 12th, that he had made new captures, and again from Corunna on November 27th, that he was "doing very well,

[1] See Allen's Naval History of the American Revolution, Vol. I, pp. 252–254.

having got Liberty to sell his prize[1] openly, and was pushing out on a fresh Cruise" (see pp. 116, 117). But all was not well. At Bilbao the time of enlistment of his crew expired. There were no funds in the hands of Gardoqui & Sons to draw upon for prize money, the men threatened open mutiny, and an outbreak actually would have occurred, had it not been for the timely arrival of one of Conyngham's prizes. "All our seamen had left the Cutter," wrote Hodge in describing this "most troublesome affair" to the American commissioners in Paris, "but the New England seamen, going on board to pursue the Tobacco Brig (see pp. 5, 119), occasioned our people to go on board likewise; but as soon as she returned, our people again left the Vessell. When I went on board, there were a greater number of prisoners than our Men, and its being an open port, I wonder that they did not take the Vessel from our people. After my going on board with six Men as a reinforcement, there was still danger, but thank God, we brought her safe into Bilboa, and I have had nothing but trouble with our people ever since. I have been obliged to settle with them for their wages and prize money, and after all one half have left the Vessell. The wages and disbursements upon the Cutter amounts to Pieces of Vellon 109,284, and the share of prize Money to the officers and crew Amounts to 137,750 Pieces of Vellon besides their share of prize Money of the ship Hope and Cargo, in which they share one third; and forty-two Volunteers who shared at the rate of one half the ship Hope, Nr. Pieces of Vellon 239,458.24, which money, together with some more I have been obliged to take up to dis-

---

[1] The ship Hope (see table facing p. 152).

charge the demands against the Cutter" (see pp. 122–124, 125).

Before the Revenge could again put to sea, however, Conyngham was obliged to change his articles, "as I could not obtain a Crew to sail under the old ones, or to engage for any term beyond a Cruize" (see p. 217). But by January, 1778, he was again on the high seas, heading WSW. and thence south along the Portuguese coast towards the Straits of Gibraltar. Seven prizes were made during this short cruise, and manned for American ports, but all but one were retaken by the British, and that one was sold by her prize-master and "Give no acct of," so that when the Revenge put into Cadiz to refit there were no funds available for the Americans to draw upon. The friendly feeling of the population towards the cause of the colonists, however, aided Conyngham out of his difficulty and enabled him to complete his preparations for another cruise, to the chagrin of the officers of the British men-of-war in the roads. "Judge of the situation of our spirited commander," wrote an officer of the Monarch on his return from Cadiz, "when during the time we lay there (seven days being detained by the wind) we had the mortification to see the usual honours paid to two Dutch frigates, and above all to the Revenge American privateer, commanded by Cunningham, who came swaggering in with his thirteen stripes, saluted the Spanish admiral, had it returned, and immediately got product; the Spaniards themselves carrying on board wood, water, fruit, and fresh provisions; all which we were eye-witnesses of, as he anchored directly under our stern, within two cables length" (see p. 127). The British tried to make a surprise attack upon the Revenge and cut her out in the dead of night, but Conyngham was warned in time of the preparations making on board the Monarch so that the attack did not materialize (see p. 6).

Returning northward, the Revenge was driven by gales into the strongly fortified seaport of Ferrol on the northwestern coast of Spain, after which she made a cruise to the southward as far as the Canary Islands and intercepted several English vessels. The brig Peace & Harmony and the brig Betsey were captured in the Atlantic, the snow Fanny off the coast of Portugal, the ship Hope and the brigs Carabonnere and Tapley in the Straits of Gibraltar, the brig Maria off Cape Finisterre, two brigs in the Bay of Biscay, and a third off the mouth of the Straits (see p. 128). And this notwithstanding "those seas covered by British Cruzers of every description and [with] orders from their Government to follow the revenge into any harbour she might be in and destroy her" (see p. 7). But Conyngham could not be caught; even in the sight of British men-of-war he continued his depredations, and on one occasion, off Cape St. Vincent, he actually brought to and burned the tender to H. B. M. S. Enterprize under the very guns of that frigate (see table facing p. 152).

All these captures were entirely regular. But from Conyngham's experiences on a previous cruise, when his men compelled him to send in a French brig, we may infer that the Revenge's crew was not always amenable to discipline or willing to abide by the laws of civilized warfare. Such an unfortunate usurpation of authority on the part of the men did, in fact, occur again in May, 1778, when the Revenge fell in with the Swedish brig Henrica Sophia, bound from London to Teneriffe. Conyngham attempted to restrain his crew, but the men would not be denied their capture. They manned the brig and ordered her to Boston, and even assumed full responsibility for their act by signing the following statement of their position in the matter: "Whereas Captn. Cunningham says that he has directions not to Insult any Neutral Flag yet, the Cargoe appearing so plain to be British property we have eng'd him to take her, & try her chance to America" (see pp. 133, 138, 139, 146–150). As soon as the news of this outrage reached Paris, the Swedish ambassador at the Court of Versailles registered his protest with the Comte de Vergennes and asked the French Court's intervention, as Sweden at that time had "no relations with the United States of America." But the French Government replied that they could give no satisfaction, as they had "no right to make representations on this subject, and still less to influence their principles and their conduct towards Powers which have not only no treaty with them, but which have not yet even recognized their independence" (see p. 139). Still, the matter did not rest there. The details of the affair were soon made known to the American commissioners in Paris through their friend Ferdinand Grand, and Franklin was thus able to disavow Conyngham's conduct and to denounce his seizure of the brig as an "act of piracy," for which "he will certainly be punished when duly prosecuted, for not only a regard to justice in general, but a strong disposition to cultivate the friendship of Spain" (see p. 147).

This unfortunate affair gave the British the opening which they had been long awaiting. Unable to cope with the swift sailing Revenge on the high seas, they had sought to close Spanish ports against her. But this they had been unable to prevail upon the Court of Madrid to do. The "American corsair" was too popular with the people. All the efforts of the British ambassador had been in vain. Then occurred the affair of the Henrica Sophia. The attitude of the Spanish Government changed almost immediately. The appeals of the British representatives suddenly found listening ears. A word, and the "offended Court" issued the requested orders against the American cutter, and Conyngham, when he sailed into the harbor of Corunna later in the spring, found the port closed to him entirely. Fortunately, an anchorage in a small neighboring inlet was allowed him by some of his friends, and here, under the bold headlands of the Galician coast, he repaired his vessel and refitted her for another cruise (see p. 7).

With no ports open to her in either of the Bourbon kingdoms, it seemed as if the Revenge's activities in European waters had come to a close. So, as soon as the vessel was again ready for sea, Conyngham, on September 1, 1778, bade farewell to his former cruising ground, and set all sail for the West Indies. During the passage across the Atlantic not a single vessel was sighted. But, once in the Caribbean, better fortune attended the lucky little cutter. Two British privateers with valuable cargoes struck their colors to her off St. Eustatia in November. Two schooners, a brig, and a sloop were captured in rapid succession and brought safely into St. Pierre. A despatch from Martinique even credited her with "an engagement off Barbadoes with a King's Cutter of 28 guns, which [she] pursued near the guns of the fort, and which would not have escaped, had it not been for an high sea which prevented boarding her" (see p. 154).

In short, as Conyngham put it, the Revenge "kept the British privateers in Good order in those seas" (see p. 9).[1]

After this, the Revenge set her course for the Delaware Capes. She made an uneventful passage. Not a sail was sighted during the voyage, and Philadelphia was reached without mishap on February 21, 1779. Here Conyngham delivered a precious cargo of arms and munitions of war to the Continental military authorities, and not long after the Revenge herself was turned over by him to the Marine Committee to be sold by them at public auction (see pp. 9, 154, 155, 157).

Thus ended the career of the cutter Revenge as a Continental vessel of war. Hers had been a glorious record. Secretly fitted out in a foreign port, she had managed, by ruse, to sail and throw off her mask under the guns of the very ships charged with preventing her departure. From that moment she began to sweep the seas of England's commerce.[2] English ships were afraid to leave their harbors. English merchants refused to load their wares except in French and Dutch bottoms. Conyngham became the most dreaded man in England. The effect of the Revenge's presence at sea was immediate. In eighteen months she captured twenty-seven English vessels and sank or burned thirty-three more. The sales of her prizes in Spain[3] realized sums which were of

[1] During this time William Bingham, the American agent in Martinique, disposed of the Revenge as a public vessel (see p. 8). She sailed under his orders, and Conyngham was required "as an Officer in the Service of the Congress" to do his bidding on several occasions (see pp. 150, 153).

[2] Arthur Lee to Samuel Adams, October 4, 1777.

[3] For the list of the prizes sold in Spanish ports by Gardoqui & Sons and Lagoanere & Company, see table facing p. 152.

great moment to the American commissioners in Europe. It is even affirmed that the money advanced to Mr. Adams for traveling expenses, when he landed in Spain from the French frigate La Sensible, a year or two later, was derived from this source (see p. 195).

But the dash and pluck of the intrepid Conyngham did even more. From the moment he returned to Dunkirk with the Harwich packet the eyes of Europe were centered upon him. His name became a catchword in the taverns of the Continent. His achievements aroused the enthusiasm of the people of the Bourbon countries. His captures embroiled the Courts of St. James and Versailles. From that moment the intervention of France in the American Revolution became an assured fact.

A few weeks after the sale of the Revenge, odd to remark, Conyngham was again on the quarter-deck of the cutter. The State of Pennsylvania had been one of the bidders at the auction, but the successful purchaser was a firm of Philadelphia merchants, who intended to use her as a privateer. For about a fortnight the Revenge was chartered by the Executive Council for the protection of the city's commerce on the river, under an agreement which included Conyngham as her commander. But by the month of April the charter expired, and Conyngham put to sea from the Capes of the Delaware, as privateersman and part owner of the Revenge, though under his former Congress commission of May 2, 1777.

Upon this cruise Conyngham's good fortune seems to have forsaken him. "I went round to New York," he writes, "laid in the roads, two privateers who followed me kept in sight—I made every effort to get them to come down, but to no effect—then made chase after them, but to no purpose—at length, as the d—l would have it, led me into the very teeth of the Gallatea (Captain Jordan). I made effort to escape, but in vain, her teeth were too many. I was taken—my crew were sent on board the prison ship in New York—I was lodged in the condemned dungeon for fourteen days."[1] (See pp. 11, 159.)

The date of the capture of the Revenge was the 27th of April, 1779. During the first week of July, Conyngham arrived in England in irons to "receive that punishment from his injured country, which his crimes shall be found to deserve" (see p. 183). What he suffered, we know from the pages of his own diary. In fact, such was his treatment, that, when the news of it reached the ears of his fellow citizens, a memorial was at once presented to the Continental Congress at Philadelphia. The accusation upon which the British authorities in New York based their action towards Conyngham was "that he had acted without a Commission when early in the year 1777 he commanded a small vessel called the Surprize and in her captured the Harwich Packet in the British Channel" (see p. 174). This charge the Marine Committee of Congress hastened to deny, adding that, unless immediate satisfaction were given, "retaliation will be made." In addition, the Secretary of Congress was directed to write to Sir George Collier, in command of his Majesty's naval forces at New York, protesting against the American captain's "rigorous and ignominious confinement" (see p. 181). But the British admiral refused "to answer demands when they

[1] Barnes's The Tragedy of the Lost Commission (in The Outlook, January 3, 1903, p. 81).

[xlviii]

are made in an uncivil way." Conyngham continued in irons, and the members of Congress were compelled to carry out their threat of retaliation by ordering the close confinement in the American prison at Boston of an officer of the Royal Navy (see pp. 184, 191).

In England, Conyngham was constantly reminded of the gallows that awaited him. "Lodgd. in the Black Hole as usall," he remarks almost daily in his prison journal. Then from Pendennis Castle at Falmouth he was transferred to Plymouth, where he was confined in Mill Prison "to stand a tryale with his most Gracious Sovering George the 3rd." "On rebel Allowance 6oz beef & 6 of bread for 24 hours," he relates, "the least fault as they termed it, 42 days in the dungeon on the half of the above allowance of beef & bread—of the worst quality. Suffered a seveare & cruel treatment, dogs, cats rats even the Grass eaten by the prisoners, thiss hard to be credited, but is a fact" (see pp. 11, 171). Twice Conyngham attempted to escape. Once he actually walked out of the prison gate in the dress of a visiting doctor. But on his third effort, on November 3, 1779, he did get away, digging himself out, with fifty-three American prisoners, and committing "treason through his majesties earth" (see p. 194). Reaching London, he found there friends and money. The authorities made every effort to apprehend him, but "the pirate" easily evaded their clutches, and after a while made his way safely to the Channel coast, whence he had little difficulty in reaching Dutch shores (see p. 11).

It happened that at this moment John Paul Jones was in the Texel with his squadron and the captured Serapis. So Conyngham placed himself under the commodore's orders and with him escaped to sea, evading the British blockading squadron on the night of December 27, 1779 (see p. 11). After a cruise in the English Channel, the Alliance ran down the Bay of Biscay, stopping first at L'Orient and then at Corunna. Here Conyngham decided to leave her, and boarded the tartan Experiment bound for the United States. Unfortunately for poor Conyngham, the Experiment was captured, on March 17, 1780, by the British Admiral Edwards, and again he found himself committed to the hardships of Mill Prison.

It was not until June, 1781, that Franklin was able to congratulate Conyngham on his safe return to French soil (see p. 205). "Proceeded to paris," writes Conyngham in his journal, "then Lorient Afterwards to Nantes," where he prepared for another cruise in the fine 24-gun ship Layona. But "the day she was Launched We had the information of peace Materials guns & Greater part of the crew engaged." So in great disappointment all plans were changed, and Conyngham returned to Philadelphia in the ship Hannibal (see p. 12).

As soon as Conyngham was free again he found himself in a peculiar position. The original commission which he had received from the American commissioners in Paris had never been returned to him after the French authorities seized his papers in May, 1777. Consequently some documents of identification had to be obtained before he could be placed "in the same Situation he was by virtue of the said Commission." So he appealed to Congress, forwarding in support of his application a copy of the certificate Franklin handed to him in Paris on August 7, 1782 (see pp. 131, 207). This memorial was favorably reported upon by the Congressional Committee of the War in October, 1783. But, for some reason, the Government deferred the settlement of the matter to a future date. So a second time Conyngham made his appeal. And then came the blow, unexpected as it was cruel, that the committee of Congress to which was referred his memorial had reported that the commission issued to him by the commissioners in Paris did "not give rank in the Navy" but had been "intended for temporary expeditions only" (see p. 209). Again and again Conyngham repeated his request, petitioning yearly, as he himself states, from 1779 to 1798. In 1793 the case came under judgment. The Secretary of the Treasury, Alexander Hamilton, assured Conyngham that a "report on the Petition, which was referred to me, will be made to Congress next session." But many of the witnesses were dead, Dr. Franklin among them. Some of the commissioners' agents turned against him. His suit for the restitution of funds owing him and back payments was held not proven (see p. 158).

During the quasi-war with France, Conyngham was in command of the armed brig Maria, of which he was part owner, and made several cruises in her, but with little success. Again, at the outbreak of the War of 1812, though advanced in years and broken in health, he endeavored to repeat the successes of his Channel ventures, but was forced to give up the attempt.

But never could he give up his fight for recognition. Year after year he sent petitions to Congress and tried to get a review of his claims. Year after year he made inquiries for his lost commission, the possession of which would have determined at once his position and rank in the navy. Twice he himself searched Paris for the precious document, but no trace of it could be found. That Conyngham could produce no proof in substantiation of his assertion was a fact upon which Benjamin Walker laid particular stress in his review of the case for the Government. The commission had not been recorded at the time of its issuance by Franklin. Even the one that he had in his possession when captured by the British in 1778 could not be produced in evidence. In vain he presented his sworn accounts, his receipts, and his bills from the Spanish agents. He received always the same answer, until at last the end came. He died in Philadelphia, on the 27th of November, 1819.[1]

[1] "The characters of the Surprise and Revenge," says Fenimore Cooper, in his Naval History of the United States, Vol. I, pp. 97–99, "appear never to have been properly understood. In all the accounts of the day, and in nearly if not in quite all the subsequent histories, these vessels are spoken of as privateers, authorized to act by the commissioners at Paris. It is not clear that the commissioners sent private armed vessels to sea at all, though the act may have come within the scope of their powers. That the two cutters commanded by Captain Conyngham were public vessels, however, is proved in a variety of ways. Like the Dolphin, 10, Lieutenant Nicholson, an officer who may be said to have almost passed his life in the navy, the Surprise and Revenge were bought and equipped by agents of the diplomatic commissioners of the United States, on public account, and the commissions granted to Captain Conyngham were gifts of personal authority, and not powers conceded to particular vessels. It is known that Dr. Franklin, at a later day, and with an especial object in view, granted temporary commissions in the navy, but there is no evidence that either of those bestowed on Captain Conyngham possessed this conditional character. The Revenge was finally given up to the Navy Board in Philadelphia, and was sold on public account. It is certainly competent for a government to consider its public vessels as it may see fit, or to put them in the several classes of vessels of war, revenue cruisers, packets, troop-ships, transports, or anything else, but it would, at least, be a novelty for it to deem any of its own active cruisers privateers. The very word would infer a contradiction in terms. Paul Jones speaks of his desire to obtain Captain Conyngham as a member

In concluding, the Editor wishes most gratefully to acknowledge the Society's appreciation of Mr. James Barnes's permission to publish the historic documents which were drawn from his collection and to reproduce the illustrations which are included in this volume. It had been hoped that Mr. Barnes would himself undertake the preparation of the Conyngham papers, but his absence abroad prevented him from fulfilling this wish.

And to the officials of the Library of Congress, the New York Public Library, the Massachusetts Historical Society, and the Bureau of Rolls and Library of the Department of State, the Editor's thanks are also due for their interest and assistance in the preparation of this history of the cruises of the Surprize and Revenge.

of a court martial, as late as 1779; and in a remonstrance against the treatment shown to Captain Conyngham, then a prisoner of war, made by Congress, through its Secretary, Charles Thompson, of the date of July, 1779, that officer is termed 'Gustavus Conyngham, a citizen of America, late commander of an armed vessel in the service of said States, and taken on board a private armed cutter,' &c. &c. Here the distinction between public and private armed vessels is unequivocally made, and the fact that Captain Conyngham had served in both is as clearly established; it being admitted that he was acting in a privateer at the precise moment of his capture. The latter circumstance in no degree affected the rank of Captain Conyngham, officers of the navy quite frequently serving in private armed ships, after the first two or three years of the war, in consequence of there not having been public vessels to afford them employment. That there was some irregularity in giving Captain Conyngham two commissions for the same rank, and bearing different dates, is true, but this arose from necessity; and want of regularity and system was a fault of the times, rather than of those who conducted the affairs of the American marine during the Revolution. There can be no reasonable doubt that both the Surprise and the Revenge were public vessels of war, and that Gustavus Conyngham was a captain in the navy of the United States of America, in virtue of two commissions granted by a competent authority; and that, too, subsequently to the declaration of independence, or after the country claimed all the political rights of sovereign power."

THE CRUISES OF
GUSTAVUS CONYNGHAM

THE CRUISES OF
GUSTAVUS CONYNGHAM

A Narrative respective Lugger surprize &
Cutter revenge.[1]

1st The Lugger[2] surprize was purchased in dunkirk
early in the Year 1777, and fitted out by order of the
Commissioners of the United States at paris, doctor
Franklin & silas dean,[3] & the appointed Agents in dunkirk for that purpose, & my commission, a Captain of
the Navy of the United States, Given to me by P. Commissioners in Paris; signed by John Hancock, then
president in Congress, dated first day of March 1777,
attested Chas. thompson Sectr. In thiss vessell made a
cruze to the East, took the harwick packett[4] & Brig
Joseph on the 3d & 4th May 1777, secured the mail &
delivered it to one of the agents on our return to dunkirk
with those prizes, which were Given up by order of the
french Government, Capt. & crew confined in prison,
my commission taken & sent up to Versailles & not re-

[1] In The Pennsylvania Magazine of History and Geography, Vol.
XXII, pp. 479–488.

[2] A small vessel carrying two or three masts, with a running bowsprit upon which she set lug-sails.

[3] The American Commissioners to the Court of France.

[4] The Prince of Orange, carrying the mails from Harwich to
Helvoetsluis in Holland.

turned—here it is to be observed the Commissioners was
not well informed as to the views of the french court or
by designe from every circumstance Led to beleive the
Latter from political motives, the court of Versailles
carried on their duplicity & blinded the British minister Lord stormount. Also that the Crew should be
delivered up, and actually sent two sloops of War &
tenders to dunkirk to receive us. 3d The revenge cutter[1] was also purchased and fitted out at dunkirk by the
same directions.[2] Viz—the Commissioner at paris &
their Agents, first a house to advance the money. 2d A
person to purchase a vessell & that in England, 3d the
material, 4th a person With a priest to execute, thiss to
shew the caution necessary at that time, and my Commission as before mentioned as a publick one—Given to
me by Wm Carmichael Sect to the commissioners at
paris, dated 2d May 1777 attested by Chas thompson
Sect. 4th Notwithstanding all this Caution & obscurity
the french Government required a surety that the revenge should not commence hostilys on the British—the
Commissioners procured an American Citizen[3] for the
purpose & Wm Carmichael[4] came to dunkirk to ex-
pedite the Cutter & gave me verbal explanations, could
not be committed to paper.[5] Also a Letter not to attack,
but if attacked at Liberty to retaliate in every manner in
our power—Burn—Sink & destroy the Enemy.[6] 5th
16th Jully 1777, the revenge left dunkirk next day at-

[1] A small vessel with one mast and a straight running bowsprit; a
class of vessel common to the Channel of England.

[2] By William Hodge, a Philadelphia merchant in the employ of the
Commissioners.

[3] William Hodge.

[4] Secretary to the American Commissioners at the Court of France.

[5] See p. 51. [6] See p. 64.

CUNNINGHAM neemt in 't Kanaal een Engelfche Paketboot.

The Taking of the Harwich Packet

tackd, fired on, chased by several british frigatts sloops of War & Cutters. Without an enquiry into the Circumstances attending the hostilety commenced, the french Government threw the Surety into the bastile,[1] further deception to appease Lord Stormount & his court for the surety was done away & the revenge at Liberty to retaliate, the coast lined by British frigatts & Cruszers of every description. A vessell in disguise in dunkirk peers to give Signals on our going out & Was executed & answered in the offing by their ships of War; 6th Count de Stang[2] was fitting a fleet at toulon by report destined for the protection of their Coloneys so he should be clear of the European seas—the real object in view. A secret, our ministers at Court urging a declaration of those intentions brought it to a close the Compt de Vergennes could no longer avoid. Count de Stang was but 24 hours late of capturing Lord howe in the delaware—

7th In the first instance of those Armaments at dunkirk it was to Capture & destroy the transports & to liberate the hessians & the other troops from the Continant bound to England, on Certain Conditions, destroy the Enemy; plan in sending those troops to America from dificulty & delay in paris & dunkirk. We lost a Glorious Opportunity.

8th Leaving dunkirk we stood to the E & N E, made several prizes in the German Ocean, N. Seas, Irish Channel & Western Ocean, destroyed several others, ordered to America, West Indes, to such places as their Cargoes would answer, few of them Got in safe, some of the prize masters made the most of them to their own

---

[1] See pp. 83 and 88.   [2] Comte d'Estaign.

use. Also by deception Arrived in England—We suffered from Gales sprung our bowsprit, short of supplys put into Kinehead—N. W. Coast of Ireland—We got Watter, verry little else to be got theare, the little we Got, paid them their own price—Leaving this place Bare away for ferrol—on our Arrival there No Agent or person Would Undertake to supply us at Corruna—the house of Lazonere & Co.[1] undertook to supply the revenge on condition of my responsibility for the payment of Advances they should make—I complyd with—

9th I wrote the Commissioners at paris Giving them every information of our cruze & our situation, Also the names of the Mercantile houses in spain our prizes should be addressed too & they approved of and appointed the house of Lazonere & Co. Consul & Agents for every Continental vessell or their prizes that should enter that port, or other ports in Gallicia—Giving me orders to cruze in those seas & where most probable to make prizes to bilboa to the house of Guardozine,[2] selecting the most difficult port they could have pointed out, Also into the hands of the principal merchts were they should arrive. We made several cruzes from Corruna & ferroll the prizes as before mentioned with directions on arriving safe—to Give every information to the Commissioners to take their directions to those houses they were addressed too—

10th in 1777 fell in with the french Brig Grasiosa of Cape Ortinzal from London bound to Corruna, a valuable Cargo amt pr Invoice 75,000 pounds sterl. covered by a Spaniard in Corruna, thiss and other circumstances

---

[1] Lagoanere & Co., the American agents at Corunna, Spain.
[2] Gardoqui & Sons, the American agents at Bilboa.

well known on board revenge. thiss vessell & cargo was fully insured in England against all. the crew insisted she should be stoptd otherways would do no further outcry, put a crew on board, ordered her to bilboa, from Gales & seveare W. arrived at St Sebastians—the officer & Crew sent to prison, french Capt & crew put in comd of the brig. On my arrival at bilboa in the revenge I went to St Sebastians by Land, then every difficulty ensued to Get our people Liberated from prison, I was obliged to submit to their terms, viz—the Governour & Secty, I protested against such arbitrary proceedings & claiming a restitution on the Spanish Govermt & left St Sebastians. 11th the spanish Governour & his secty by representations to Court recd orders to discharge the Brig, they disposed of the Cargo, pay the french Capt. the freight & proceed as he saw fit, he refitted, that they had no right either to detaine the vessell or make sale of the Cargo. After Long delay the Spanish Court determined that the Captors should pay the damages in fourteen days from the date of said decission, if not paid by them in that time, the french Capt should pay it, so much for diplomatick proceedings. A concerted plan of Villany at Court & St Sebastians; it is to be observed the time specifyd by the Spanish Courts that the Captor should pay they was out of their power & they knew it. —Appearance of a public sale md of thiss Cargo & St. Sebastians, the Greater part of purchased for that Governour & secy most arbitrary & clandestine manner.

12th at Bilboa the time the crew was engaged for Expired, no provision made for paying them off the Agent theare had no funds for that purpose. one of our prizes Getting in safe at Bilboa otherways would have been attended with disagreeable circumstances. A crew consisting of all nations not possible to Govern or be Governed, short of mutiny in several instances, Afterwards could not engage a crew for any term beyond a Cruze & to be settled with at the expiration of—No Wages pr month, a bounty advanced to be deducted from their shares in prizes as pr orders of Congress, & regulation of seaman. 13th 1778 left bilboa on a Cruze to the Wt S W. & So strights of Tib, made several prizes, sent some to [America], & different ports in Europe, few Got in safe. Seven prizes ordered to Am. all retaken but one, that the prize master sold and Give no acct of, we were badly situated for prize master.

14th put into Cadiz to refit & apply to the house of Lacoute & Co. no funds there. A prize getting in we were able to refit & proceed on a cruze to the Wt N. E— & No Lattd 50° No made prizes & destroyd several, had a bad Acct of their fate som of them we never heard of, An English ship of the Line & two frigatts were laying in Cadiz on our arrival—in their usual & diabolick mode of Warfare had determined in the Night by their boats to set the revenge on fire—A Good french man on board one of them Gave notice to the french Consul of their designe, who advised us of. Consequently was prepared for them, they did appear in the dead of the night but took Care to Keep their distance, the spanish admirall had thiss notice & he politely offered a 74 Gun ship to protect us—We acknowledge the favor, but was noways apprehensive of any danger, to the 15th Contrary it was our wish they would make the Attempt. from several Gales & short supplys put into ferrol— fitted out, Went on a Cruze to the Western & Canary Islds, made severall prizes & destroyd others ordered as before observed to AM. & ports of Europe—came to

Anchor at Punto Nego, tenerif, to Wood & Watter, Also how we should be recd at the Capitol, received notice we should be received with hospitality, proceeded to Sandy-Cruze, Got provisions & Necessarys— the house of Cassalon & Co furnished us—here we learned that one of our prizes—Cargo Wine, fruit & Oyle, was at Island of Palma, the prize master was disposing of the Cargoe in League With the British Consul, We proceeded to sd Island & found he had disposed of the Cargoe, a part delivered, took the Necessary steps, Got possession of the vessell & that part of Cargo on board, with thiss obliged to be satisfyd—put a crew on board, ordered her to Martinique. 16th We Left palma, Went on a cruze to the N W. N. E & So made some prizes retaken & others no account of. those seas covered by British Cruzers of every description and orders from their Govermt to follow the revenge into any harbour she might be in & destroy her. for prizes none could be Got in, the cruze being finished put into Corruna—thear was orders from spanish Govermt that we should not be protectd or admittd General O'Neal the Commd Officer was friendly to us, Also the Cause of our Country—Gave us Liberty to proceed to puntodema a private harbour in Gallicia & refit & be supplyd in future to avoid the ports in Gallicia, every difficulty in our Way by British influence at Court & infamous representations of their Consuls the Agents by order Commison made the Advances—

17th rec'd a Letter from Arthur Lee Esq. informing he was sole commison for Spain. I wrote him in Answer & Gave him the same information as I had the commison at paris, viz. the Names & firms of those houses the prizes were orderd or would arrive & he might direct

[7]

as he saw fit—and he did Write the agents & orderd.
17th On arrival of prizes my directions to the prize
masters & agents they should advise the Commison &
take their orders in disposal of the property, Arthur
Lee Esq did write the Agents that all prizes made by
Continental vessells; the funds to be held at his disposal,
the revenge, no other vessell had any prizes or funds, to
the contrary continental vessells of War putting into
ports in Gallicia in want of repairs and supplys—Also
citizens of the U. S. of America, captured in those seas
put on shore coast of Gallicia, Vigo & elsewhere in the
greatest distress by british cruzers—also his excellency
John Adams on his way to paris recd Moneys at Corruna and at Bayone, All those expenses & charges from
the funds of the revenge, cutter, will be found to be no
small amount, not a word from the Commisrs of any
funds or Credit being ordered to pay any expenses that
might occur, without considering the Great Expense
attending a Cruzer, and at that day our flag under many
difficulty. 18th We left punto-dema, the Consul Lazonere settled with the crew in 1778, under articles of
agreement same as the last & proceeded for the West
Indies, advising the Commisrs of the difficultys we
Laboured under—Arrived at Martinique, made no
prizes—William Bingham Esq AM. agent theare disposed of P. cutter revenge as a publick vessell—viz. the
crew engaged for a cruze, bounty advanced them, to be
deductted from their prize money & settled with when
finished in same manner as at bilboa and had continued
in, made several cruzes to Windward & among the
Islands—made some prizes of little value, protected
several AM. merchantmen & convoyed others clear of

the Island. Kept the British privateers in Good order in those seas, Captured two of them—

19th left Martinique in 1779 arrived shortly after in Febry. philaa—the Navy board took the direction of P. Cutter & sold her at public sale by an act of Congress 12' March '79—I petition Congress for a settlement of my Acct & they refered to Alexander Hamilton Esqr Secty of State my accounts & vouchers of every description, and he promised should be reportted on first Session of Congress—he did not, petition after petition to Congress time after time to decr 26th 1797 to no Effect.

20th Some time after Peace by an order of Congress a commercial Agent was appointed to settle every account relative to the public in Europe & did call or Write to every house or agent Concerned with the revenge, cutter, for that purpose, through the Agency of William Carmichal at Madrid.

GUSTAVUS CONYNGHAM.

By a resolve of Congress, that the Capt of any single ship or armed vessel have two twentieth parts of his share, but if more ships or armed vessels be in Company when a prize is taken then the two twentieth parts to be divided amongst all the said Captains;

I went on a voyage from Philaa in the Brig charming peggy to Europe to procure Munitions of War of every description—arrived at dunkirk after circuitous route, here we could not accomplish in any way our object— the Agent Jont Nesbett[1] Went to holland & procured every article desired & ordered in philaa our vessell could not take such a cargo on board there, if possible

[1] Jonathan Nesbitt.

no person would or could undertake it—such must be procured in holland the only alternative to ship P. goods on board two dutch vessells in the Texel—the powder—saltpetter & such in one vessell, the other vessell Arms—flints medecine, cloathing & to avoid accidents to be put on board our vessell Nieuport roads, on our getting there the dutch men as usuall had not arrived, a Gale came on were obliged to slip our Cables & run into the Canal leading to Nieuport about 2½ miles from the town 4 days after the dutch men arrived We took out their Cargoes, detained by contrary winds in a canal & other difficultys at the entrance of the canal its requisite to have a fair wind—the tide so rapid otherwise carryd on the sand banks, here I am sorry to say an Irishman sailor on board the name of brackenridge is father usher to a school in Londonderry under a Mr Ewing—dezertted & Got to Ostend informed the British Consul of every particular in consequence we were stopd arrested, a guard put on board in 3 days after a light air wind & fair in our turn We put the Guard under arrest took their arms proceeding out, fell calm air of Wind came right in our case became desperate—took to our boats left the agent to claim as he did not appeare to have any hand in it, a deception should we faile—breaking an arrest under that despotick Govermt not to be trifled wh that verry guard md Oath that the agent was in same state as themselvs after this a long & tedious business took place the vessell & Cargoe damaged through ignorance of the balief; burgomaster, fisherman Wt Embezzlement a valuable cargo & vessell turned out to nothing when solde from the different charges costs & by that corrupt Govermt under the sanction of their Court & their prince Charles

—I remained in dunkirk & after-wards took the Comd of the Surprize, also after the revenge, as related in the Narative.   G: CONYNGHAM.

March 1779, the Cutter revenge being purchased by individuals—I continued in Comd of her—Went on a cruze under my former Commission U. S. Navy—taken carried into N. York[1]—sent to England in a packett in Irons Wt 55 lbs, arrived at Falmouth, pen-dominis Castle[2] & figure of 4 hand Irons added to the others, sent to plymouth committed on the high treason Act to stand a tryale with his most Gracious Sovering George the 3rd—on rebel Allowance 6oz beef & 6 of bread for 24 hours, the least fault as they termed it, 42 days in the dungeon on the half of the above allowance of beef & bread—of the worst quality. Suffered a seveare & cruel treatment for number years, dogs, cats rats even the Grass eaten by the prisoners, thiss hard to be credited, but is a fact—After Burgoine's & Cornwallis Capture, same allowance, but a little better treated, not so often reminded of the Gallows, After several attempts to escape from prison, as often brought back, at last Got to texel Went on board the Alliance frigatt paul Jones comd proceeded on a cruze down channel & towards the Western Islands put into Corruna to refit Supplyd by Messrs Lazonere & Co.—here I went on board the tartan.[3]

Experiment bound to the U S N. on the 17 day of March captured by the Admiral Edwards private cruze carryed to dartmouth from theare to Mill prison[4]

---

[1] See pp. 158, 160.   [2] Pendennis Castle.
[3] A small one-masted coasting vessel common to the Mediterranean.
[4] This prison was situated on a promontory, projecting into the

Lodge, as usual dungeon recovering from a seveare sickness, some time after made my escape Got over to Ostend proceeded to paris then Lorient Afterwards to Nantes, Layona ship to mount 24 twelves and Nines, the day she was Launched We had the information of peace Materials guns & Greater part of the crew engaged— Citizens of the US of AM coming to Nantes numbers every day in the greatest distress—no provision made for them actually begging for a morsel of bread— Jonathan Williams and Jonathan Nisbett did every thing in the power of man for their releive. We took on board the ship hannibal 95 as we posible could and the crew 35 men no Wages, Landed them at Philaa, Without any charge to them or the Govermt thiss very differt from the Conduct of many other AM Vessells in that port & other ports in france at that time—

G. CONYNGHAM.

Sound, between Plymouth and Plymouth Dock, two considerable towns: it lies on the right hand, as you go from Dock to Plymouth, and about an equal distance from either. Formerly there stood windmills on this eminence, which circumstance gave it the name of "Mill Hill;" hence the prison was called "Mill Prison." There were three buildings, one of which had been built in Queen Anne's time, as tradition informs us. The largest building was a hundred feet long and about twenty feet wide; situated at the north end of the yard. It was two stories high, built with stone and lime, having no windows on the north front. There was a space of about twenty feet between this building and the Commissary's office, which stood to the west, but had no windows in the east end. A wall on the north as high as the eaves of the prison, extended from the prison to the office; a similar wall on the south, joined the two buildings. In this wall was a gate leading into the main yard. (From The New England Historical and Genealogical Register, 1865, Vol. XIX, p. 74.)

Other interesting particulars may be found in the Memoirs of Andrew Sherburne, who was for some time confined in this prison (pp. 81–89).

[THE AMERICAN COMMISSIONERS TO THE
COMMITTEE OF CORRESPONDENCE[1]]

(Extract)

Paris, March 12th. 1777

In ours of Feb. 6 of which a Copy is enclosed, we acquainted you that we are about purchasing some Cutters to be employed as Packet Boats. We have succeeded in getting one from Dover in which we propose to send our present Dispatches.—Mr. Hodge who went to Dunkirk & Flushing, where he thought another might be easily found, has not yet acquainted us with his Success.

[THE AMERICAN COMMISSIONERS TO THE COMMITTEE
OF CORRESPONDENCE[2]]

(Extract)

Paris, March 12th. 1777

Mr. Hodge writes us that he has provided another Cutter. We intended to employ one of them as a Packet, but several of yours being now here, and haveing lately made a Contract for sending one every Month, a Copy of which we enclose, we shall make use of this new Purchase as a Cruiser.

[1] Stevens's Facsimiles, Vol. XIV, No. 1448–1.
[2] *Ibid.*, No. 1448–9.

[SILAS DEANE TO CONRAD A. GERARD[1]]

Sir,—   Paris, March 22d, 1777.

Enclosed is a letter from his Excellency, which I pray you to deliver. I have also troubled you with a short Memoir on the subject I had the honor of mentioning to you the other day, and pray you would send me a line, informing me whether the petition of Mr. Cunningham can be granted, and what will be the expences attending it. As he proposes going out of town soon, I am the more urgent for an early answer.

                    I have the honor, etc.

Monsr. Gérard.[2]   S. DEANE.

Memoir

Mr. Cunningham, a gentleman of family & fortune in Ireland, who has been for many years respectably established in business in Philadelphia, is about to settle at Martinico, for carrying on to the greatest advantage commerce between France and the United States of America, for which reason he is desirous of being naturalized in this Kingdom. He is a protestant by religious profession, but will ever make it his study to maintain the character, he has hitherto universally held, of a peaceable and useful member of society. As his business obliges him soon to leave Paris, he prays to be

[1] In The Deane Papers, Collections of the New-York Historical Society, Vol. II, p. 31.

[2] Later, in 1778, the first Minister Plenipotentiary of France to the United States. He sailed from Toulon, on April 13, 1778, with the Comte d'Estaign's fleet.

informed whether his petition can be granted, and what are the forms & modes of proceeding necessary to be attended to.

Paris, March 22d, 1777.

[GEORGE LUPTON[1] TO WILLIAM EDEN[2][3]]

Wednesday Evening
[30 April, 1777]

Dear Sir

The present serves to acknowledge the receipt of your esteemed favour of 25th Current, but as I have very little time to spare, shall not enter into Particulars, save I must mention the last dispatches was under my care for near two hours, while Conyngham was Preparing himself for his intended Journey, of course you 'll see it was possiable for me to have come of with same, but you may depend I shall not enter into those schemes rashly, unless a finishing stroke could be done by same,—at same time I flatter myself I can be of more consequence to you here, than if you was made acquainted with the Contents of one of them, therefore shall follow your advice and act very cautiously on those delicate points— Mr. Deane dines today with the Countess D'anville & is very intimate with the Vice Admiral of France, the Count   his name I recollect not at present,— Shall answer your letter very fully by the next Courier. Adieu! Good Sir, & believe Yours Sincerely

G.. L..

[1] An Englishman in France watching the course of events.
[2] Of the British Foreign Office in London.
[3] Stevens's Facsimiles, Vol. II, No. 147–4.

[LORD STORMONT[1] TO LORD WEYMOUTH[2][3]]

Paris Thursday Morning
May 8th. 1777

My Lord

Last night I received the enclosed Letter from Mr. Frazer which at his desire was sent from Calais by Express. I thought the Business too important to brook Delay and therefore went this Morning to Versailles I waited first on M. de Vergennes[4] and began by saying that I was sorry to trouble him but that I was come to speak to him upon a Subject of a very serious Nature I added that I should confine myself to bare Matter of Fact leaving it to his Excellency to make those Reflections *qui se presenteroient la dessus en foule* after this Short Preface which sufficiently Raised his Attention I stated the Facts as they were Stated to me by Mr. Frazer[5] and at the same time delivered to Him a Short note which was nothing but a Repetition of what I had said. M. de Vergennes seemed surprized and answered with great seeming Frankness that this was a case where it was unnecessary to make *des Representations* and that *le simple exposé du fait* was sufficient. I replied that I was so convinced of this that both in what I had said to him and what I had given in writing I had simply stated the fact without accompanying it with any Re-

---

[1] The British Ambassador to the Court of France.
[2] Secretary of State for the Southern Department.
[3] Stevens's Facsimiles, Vol. XV, No. 1529–1, 5.
[4] Louis XVI's Minister of Foreign Affairs.
[5] The British Inspector of Fortifications at Dunkirk. See p. 20.

In CONGRESS.

The Delegates of the United Colonies of New-Hampshire, Massachusetts Bay, Rhode-Island, Connecticut, New-York, New-Jersey, Pennsylvania, the Counties of New-Castle, Kent, and Sussex on Delaware, Maryland, Virginia, North-Carolina, South-Carolina, and Georgia, to _Gustavus Cunningham_,

WE reposing especial Trust and Confidence in your Patriotism, Valour, Conduct and Fidelity, DO by these Presents, constitute and appoint you to be _Commander_ _Jno_ in the service of the Thirteen United Colonies of North-America, fitted out for the defence of American Liberty, and for repelling every hostile Invasion thereof. You are therefore carefully and diligently to discharge the Duty of _Commander_ _in D. x D Off. L_ by doing and performing all Manner of Things thereunto belonging. And we do strictly charge and require all Officers, Marines and Seamen under your Command, to be obedient to your Orders as _rroled by Congress_ And you are to observe and follow such Orders and Directions from Time to Time, as you shall receive from this or a future Congress of the United Colonies, or Committee of Congress, for that Purpose appointed, or Commander in Chief for the Time being of the Navy of the United Colonies, or any other your superior Officer, according to the Rules and Discipline of War, and the Usage of the Sea, and the Instructions herewith given you, in Pursuance of the Trust reposed in you. This Commission to continue in Force until revoked by this or a future Congress.

By Order of the Congress

John Hancock President.

Augs. Chstnerronfuy

Baltimore
March 1st 1777

The Lost Commission, March 1, 1777

flexion, any Demand; being persuaded that it was better to leave this Court to do instantly of their own accord what their Wisdom and Justice could not fail to prompt upon such an occasion. He thanked me, said that such proceedings were certainly not to be suffered *et qu'on y mettroit bien ordre.* He then asked me If I did not mean to see M. de Maurepas and upon my telling Him I did, he said he would immediately follow me thither that we might settle this affair. I was scarce sat down at M. de Maurepas[1] when M. de Vergennes came in and Read the Note I had given Him. M. de Maurepas said without a Moments hesitation that it was an irregular unlawful proceeding which must not be suffered and that orders must be sent immediately to Dunkirk. He then joked a little upon the pretty Spot of work such fellows would make if they were not kept in awe, and ended with begging that M. de Vergennes would go to M. de Sartine[2] to have an order sent by Express to Stop and Examine the Pirate and set at Liberty the Prizes He had taken. I desired that the order might mention Prizes in the Plural Number thinking this a necessary Precaution to include the Packet if she has been brought into Dunkirk or any other Prizes that might have been taken since the Date of Mr. Frazers Letter. I did not till my Return from Versailles know the Pirates Name which Mr. Frazer mentioned in his first Letter by Post that is just arrived. I see he is an American Cunningham. This however makes no material difference as the Arming a Vessel in the french Kings Ports going from thence to cruize against us and

[1] The French Prime Minister.
[2] The French Minister of Marine.

returning thither as to an Asylum is clearly contrary to all Rule and inconsistent with the friendship between the two Courts as M. de Vergennes himself readily allowed.

I took this opportunity My Lord of mentioning to M. de Maurepas and M de Vergennes the Instructions sent to Lord Grantham with which they seemed highly satisfied. M de Vergennes then left us to go to M de Sartines but desired first to speak for a Moment to M de Maurepas who immediately returned to me and in his chearful way said well, My Lord I hope you will allow that we are very ready to do you Justice and that we did not take *much time* to deliberate. I told him he had done Exactly what I expected and that I purposely came to Him before the Messenger set out that by the same Dispatch that mentioned this incident I might be able to add that the Evil was cured. He thanked me and we parted very good friends. I must do Him and M de Vergennes the Justice to say that nothing could be franker than their behaviour on this occasion or readier than the Promises they made—I hope they will be exactly fulfilled.

I am with the greatest Truth and Respect
My Lord
Your Lordships
most obedient
humble servant
STORMONT

P.S. I send your Lordship inclosed an extract of a letter a friend of mine received from St. Malo.

[MONTMORENCY, PRINCE DE ROBECQ, TO THE
COMTE DE VERGENNES[1]]

(Translation)

Sir   Dunkirk, 9th. May 1777

I had the honour of reporting to you yesterday what happened in the port of this town relative to the prizes taken by one Cunningham, an American corsair. I have now that of sending you the copy of the judicial and extra-judicial declarations which that man has made, to which I annex the résumé of the explanations which I have been able to procure relative to another small vessel which is being prepared in this port, and which the English Commissary, who is here, suspects of wishing to carry on privateering against the vessels of his nation. The look-out man, who is on the tower of this town, has this moment informed me that the two small vessels of the King of England which were anchored yesterday in sight of this port to examine what was going on, and which, at the evening tide, cast anchor in the Fosse du Mardick, had just fired a gun to cause two small vessels which had just left here to lay to, that they launched a small boat to go and examine them, that they remained about a quarter of an hour on board, and that they afterwards allowed them to go on their way.

Details on the subject of the American vessel which brought into Dunkirk an English packet going to Helvoetsluys and the restitution of which had been ordered.

I was about to finish this letter, Sir, when M. de Villers, Naval Commissary, communicated to me the orders which M. de Sartine has addressed to him, and brought me the courier who handed me the letter which

[1] Stevens's Facsimiles, Vol. XV, No. 1530–1, 3.

the Minister wrote to M. de Chaulieu, the Commandant of this fortress, who is absent, and which I opened. In consequence of the orders it contained, I gave assistance to the Naval Commissary, who has just arrested the two officers and almost all the crew of the American privateer, and has placed sentinels, with which I caused him to be furnished, to guard this privateer and its two prizes, which it is impossible to release at present, as they each have a leak, and all the people who formed the crew have been sent to sea on a Dutch vessel, which has landed them in Holland. There consequently remains not a single man to resume possession of them, which will oblige M. de Villers to have them guarded, until on the intimation which the Court or Lord Stormont will give concerning them in England, someone is sent to whom they may be handed over.

I have the honour to be with sincere and inviolable attachment,   Sir,

Your very humble and
very obedient Servant
MONTMORENCY PCE. DE ROBECQ.

P.S. I do not know in what form Mr. Frazer presented the complaint to Lord Stormont, but I have reason to believe that the account which he gave him by the courier whom he sent was a little exaggerated, and that, on this occasion he overstepped the limits of the commission, the only object of which is the execution of the Treaty of Utrecht.[1]

[1] Which contained a stipulation, revived in the year 1763 by a special article in the Treaty of Paris, that no fortifications should be erected by France at Dunkirk on the front which faced the sea,—for the enforcement of which article England maintained at that port an Inspector of Fortifications.

[SILAS DEANE TO CONRAD A. GERARD[1]]

Paris 11 May 1777.

Sir

Agreable to my proposal last Evening I now have the honor of sending you this by Mr. Carmichael, impatient to know what is the Fate of Capt Cunningham, I pray you to inform me by Mr. Carmichael if he is, or is not Arrested, and whether any other of the Officers or Crew are Arrested—Also whether the Prize may be permitted to quit the Port. The Report of Capt. Cunninghams not being an American Subject but of Ireland is groundless—he has lived many years in America, is a Citizen of Philadelphia & had property there as well as a Wife & Children there born in America—it is true he was born in Ireland which is the case of many of the most respectable Inhabitants of that City with whom Capt. Cunningham has always been Concerned in Business, what may have occasioned the Report, was his passing for an Irishman sometime since in holland to extricate himself from some Difficulties to which Americans are now immediately liable at the present Time— The Facts then really are, that an American purchased a Vessel in England, took in Warlike Stores at Dunkirk Armed his Vessel at Sea, & having a Commission from the United States made two prizes, with which he imprudently returned to Dunkirk—I acknowledge he was very much to blame for this last Act, but have no ap-

---

[1] Stevens's Facsimiles, Vol. III, No. 690–1, 2.

prehension that in Consequence he can be held as a Pirate.

I have the honor to be with the most profound respect Sir your most Obedt &
Very Humbl. Servt.
S Deane.

PS since writing the Above I recd. a Lettr. from Bayonne, which is dated May 5th. & says A Vessel is arrived at Bilboa in twenty four Days from Boston which says that Genl. Howe after joining Lord Cornwallis had been obliged to retreat to New York with great Loss, that the Amphitrite was arrived in America,[1] & the People of the United States, unanimous in their high Spirits.

[GEORGE LUPTON TO WILLIAM EDEN[2]]

(Extract)

Dear Sir,   Paris, May 13th. 1777

I am still without any of your favours save the first, but flatter myself this night will do me that honour I have at last with some certainty discovered the intended voyages of Nicholson, Weakes, & Johnson,[3] they have all sail'd from Nantes, and mean if possible to intercept some of your transports with foreign troops, but in what place or latitude cannot say, this plan has been laid long

[1] At Portsmouth in April, 1777, with a valuable cargo of military stores.
[2] Stevens's Facsimiles, Vol. II, No. 158–1.
[3] Commanding the Continental cruisers Reprisal, Lexington, and Dolphin.

while, & the original one was, that Capt. Conyngham who brought the packet into Dunkirk some days since, should have intercep'd the transports when they were crossing the channel for England as they had no Convoy for protection of same, but the plan was laid aside, as they could not purchase a Vessell of sufficient force, —a Mr. Hodge has been the acting person on this occasion, he fitted out Capt. Conyngham Vessell, & he tells me he has got another of much larger force,[1] therefore it behoves you to be very Carefull and keep a constant watch on him, I dont imagine she will sail from Dunkirk but 'twill be from some of the Neighbouring ports, —this affair has made a great noise here, & I believe you may depend on having the same delivered up,—Carmichael was with Murepas[2] at Varseilles on Sunday last, but from what he tells me they are much displeased at Capt. Conynghams carrying the prizes into Dunkirk, they say if he had brought them into Havre or any other port, it would not have been taken notice of, if Lord Stormont makes a formal demand the same will be return'd, unless they should be so wanton as to burn them which have heard hinted at, but cannot imagine 't will be done—For God sake be careful of your packets which pass from Dover to Calais, as there is a plan laid of intercepting them, this I have heard hinted, and doubt not but the attempt will be made, therefore the officers of packets ought to have strict orders to sink the mail immediately on the approach of any vessell that carries the Appearance of a Rebel privateer. I only mean to give my advice, and with the greatest submission say, it ought to be adopted, but must submit to your better judgment.

[1] The Revenge.   [2] M. de Maurepas, the French Prime Minister.

[SILAS DEANE TO M. GÉRARD[1]]

(Extract)

14 May 1777

Sir

We attended your advice by Mr. Carmichael respecting the Letters, & have now directed him to wait on you to know if you can give Us any further intelligence respecting the unhappy Affair at Dunkirk—unhappy for Us, but most fortunate for Our Enemies, if Capt. Cunningham & his Crew are to be treated as Pirates, as it will be by confirming the report industriously spread at this Time in England of the Disposition of the Court, confirm the Credit of the Ministry, and by raising the Stocks, eventually procure to them, the substantial aid of Millions for the next Campaign. The within is a true extract from the Amounts we have received from America express, on which I cannot but make one reflection, I wish you to Communicate the Same, to his Excellency, the *Comte de Vergennes.*

[GEORGE III TO LORD NORTH[2]]

St. James's, May 14th, 1777.
58 min. pt. M.

Lord North,—

The preparing for the business of the House of Commons this day will naturally prevent your coming here; I therefore think it right to apprise you that the Post

[1] Stevens's Facsimiles, Vol. III, No. 692–1.
[2] Printed in the Correspondence of King George III with Lord North, Vol. II, p. 68.

Office have received notice from the agent at Dover that news is come by a letter from Captain Frazer at Dunkirk, that Cunningham, the commander of the pyratical vessel that seized the Prince of Orange packet-boat, is thrown into prison, and the said pacquet-boat and the other prizes ordered by the Court of France to be restored. This is so strong a proof that the Court of Versailles mean to keep appearances, that I think the news deserves a place in the speech you will make.

[LORD STORMONT TO LORD WEYMOUTH[1]]

(Extract)

My Lord   Paris May 14th. 1777

Yesterday morning I had the Honour of your Lordships Letter No. 34, with its several inclosures, relative to a Business, which is now upon the point of being terminated, and I hope to your entire satisfaction. Before I went to M. de Vergennes (who received me yesterday at his House in Town) I was informed that the Promise, He, and M de Maurepas made me, had been punctually fulfilled, The Moment I came into Him, he asked me with a smile, if I had received Letters from Dunkirk, and without waiting for an answer, said, that the courier was returned, that part of the Orders he carried were executed already, as the Pirate Captain and his crew were in actual custody, and that the Packet, and the Brig, should be immediately delivered, but that a proper Person must be appointed by us, to receive them. He proposed to me, that I should write to Mr. Frazer

[1] Stevens's Facsimiles, Vol. XV, No. 1531–1, 2.

to desire Him, *de sentendre avec le Commandant de Dunkerque,* with regard to the delivery of these Vessels. I readily agreed to this, and have accordingly written the enclosed Letter to Mr. Frazer. M de Vergennes said, that it was a satisfaction to them, to find, that there was not a single frenchman on board the Pirate.

[LORD STORMONT TO LORD WEYMOUTH[1]]

(Extract)   Paris May 14, 1777

The success of my application with regard to the Dunkirk Pirate has been highly displeasing to Franklin and Deane. They made strong remonstrances but were given to understand that there are some things too glaring to be winked at, and that this was a point in which they could not be supported.

[PAUL WENTWORTH[2] TO THE EARL OF SUFFOLK[3][4]]

(Extract)   [About 15 May, 1777]

I do not ground my opinion on the happy issue of the very able & dextrous management of Lord Stormont in the Dunkirk business, to which only, & not to the good disposition of this Court, is due the success which has followed that affair—

[1] Stevens's Facsimiles, Vol. XV, No. 1533-2.
[2] An American in the employ of the British ministry.
[3] Secretary of State.
[4] Stevens's Facsimiles, Vol. III, No. 694-2.

[COMTE DE SAINT GERMAIN[1] TO THE COMTE
DE VERGENNES[2]]

(Translation)

Versailles 15th May 1777.

Details concerning the
American vessel which
has brought to Dunkirk a
packet going to Hellevoetsluys

I have the honour to send you, Sir, a letter which I
have received from the Prince de Robecq containing
fresh details concerning the American privateer which
has brought two English prizes into the port of Dunkirk. I think it my duty to communicate it to you, and
I shall be much obliged to you if you will return it to
me with your opinion.

I have the honour to be with very perfect attachment,
Sir, your very humble and very obedient Servant.

SAINT GERMAIN.

M. le Comte de Vergennes

[1] The Minister of War.
[2] Stevens's Facsimiles, Vol. XV, No. 1534.

Memoranda of Some of Lord Stormont's
Correspondence[1]

18 May 1777 Lord Stormont to Lord Weymouth No. 90:—Encloses a letter from Andrew Frazer at Dunkirk which announces the arrival of the Ranger and Greyhound cutter and that an officer from each came on shore to learn the particulars of the American pirate and his prizes, and states also, that these vessels had fired shots at an English collier coming into port, which incident is regarded by the French officials in Dunkirk as a serious insult.

[GEORGE LUPTON TO WILLIAM EDEN[2]]

(Extract) 22 May 1777

This Monsieur Poulze told Moylan that the putting the Crew of Conynghams Vessell into prison was only a temporary affair, and no more than a Cloak for their other Actions & that they would be released in a very short time, but hope you'll put a stop to that; the French are very much against War with England at present (indeed its their Interest) and would suffer almost anything sooner than break with you—

[1] Stevens's Facsimiles, Vol. XV, No. 1544–8.
[2] *Ibid.,* Vol. III, No. 696–4.

[M. DE SARTINE TO THE COMTE DE VERGENNES[1]]

(Extract—Translation)

Versailles, 22 May 1777.

Extracts annexed of letters from
the Admiralty at Dunkirk on the
subject of the American privateer
which had brought in there two
English packets which it had seized.

You know, Sir, what has taken place at Dunkirk, and
the orders given there on the occasion of the armament carried out in that place of a vessel, which, having left the port under the English flag, returned to
it the next day under another name than that which it
had on leaving, and which brought in, as prizes; two
English vessels, I have the honour to send you extracts
of letters[2] which I have received from the Officers of
the Admiralty of that port, and from the Commissary in
Ordinary of Ports and Arsenals, who is performing
there the functions of director in the absence of the
Commissary General, from which you will see that
several vessels of the King of England, which have cast
anchor before the said port, not only fired on vessels of
their own nation which were leaving or entering it, but
even on French vessels; such a proceeding, in general,
taking place in a roadstead, and before a port, will
doubtless appear to you, as it does to me, very extraordinary, but especially at a moment when it was not
known what orders the King had just given.

[1] Stevens's Facsimiles, Vol. XV, No. 1537-1.
[2] Mentioned, but not given.

Memoranda of Some of Lord Stormont's Correspondence[1]

25 May 1777 Lord Stormont to Lord Weymouth:—
Enclosing copy of his letter to Vergennes transmitting
an extract of Frazer's letter relative to Cunningham's
prizes, and of the answer by Vergennes, which acknowledges receipt of the extract and states that the orders
given for the restitution of the prizes has been delayed
by transference from the Commissary of the Marine to
the judge of the Admiralty.

[THE AMERICAN COMMISSIONERS TO THE COMMITTEE OF FOREIGN AFFAIRS[2]]

(Extract)   Paris May 25, 1777.

The points principally in view are (besides the acknowledgment of American independency) an open
port for German commerce, and the permission of fitting out armed vessels to annoy the enemy's northern
trade, and of bringing in and selling our prizes. If
these points can be obtained we are assured we might
soon have a formidable squadron there, and accumulate
seamen to a great amount. The want of such a free

[1] Stevens's Facsimiles, Vol. XV, No. 1544–8.
[2] *Ibid.*, No. 1540–1, 2.

Port appears in the late instance of Capt. Cunninghams arrest at Dunkirk with the Prizes he brought in. For though the fitting out may be covered and concealed by various pretences so at least as to be winked at by Government here, because those pretences afford a good example for not preventing it, yet the bringing in of Prizes by a Vessel fitted out, is so notorious an act, and so contrary to Treaties, that if suffered it must occasion an immediate War.—Cunningham will however through favour be discharged with his Vessel as we are given to understand, but we must put up with the loss of the Prizes which being reclaimed will be restored. This is an occasion of Triumph to our Enemies which we must suffer them to enjoy for the present, assured as we are by the most Substantial Proofs of the Friendship of this Court and of Spain, which we are persuaded will soon manifest itself to all the World. The latter has already remitted to us a large sum of money as you will see by Mr. Lee's Letters, & continues to send Cargoes of supplies of which you have herewith sundry accounts. Many of these transactions are by some means or other known in England which does not resent them at present, but the opinion of an approaching War gains ground every day.

[FRANKLIN AND DEANE TO THE COMMITTEE OF
FOREIGN AFFAIRS[1]]

Paris, May 26, 1777.

Gentlemen:

The Navy of the United States, increasing in the number of its ships and force, it is of the utmost importance to direct the cruises of the ships of war, which belong either to the States or individuals, so as to annoy and alarm the enemy the most effectually, and at the same time to encourage our brave officers and seamen by the value of prizes. The West India trade was so intercepted the last season that, besides endangering the credit of every West India house in England, and absolutely ruining many, greatly helped towards sinking the revenues of Great Britain, which it was confidently asserted the other day in the House of Commons, and was not contradicted by the minister, had sunk the last year nearly one million below the usual incomes. This trade can not be attacked the coming season to equal advantage, as it will not be by any degree so large, and will be armed and under convoy. But as the commerce of Great Britain is very extensive, good policy dictates that we attack it in more than one sea, and on different coasts. The navy of Great Britain is not sufficiently numerous to infest the whole coast of North America, and at the same time guard their own, much less protect and convoy their trade in different seas.

We have not the least doubt but that two or three of

[1] MSS. Department of State; printed in Wharton's Diplomatic Correspondence of the American Revolution, Vol. II, pp. 325–327.

the Continental frigates, sent into the German ocean, with some lesser swift-sailing cruisers, might intercept and seize great part of the Baltic and northern trade, could they be in those seas by the middle of August at farthest; and the prizes will consist of articles of the utmost consequence to the States. One frigate would be sufficient to destroy the whole of the Greenland whale fishery, or take the Hudson Bay ships returning. In a word, they are unsuspicious and unguarded on that quarter, and the alarm such an expedition would give must raise the insurance in England at least twenty per cent., since Captain Cunningham's adventure occasioned ten percent to be given on the packet boats from Dover to Calais. Captain Cunningham having been put in prison, and the prizes restored, they are again lulled into security; the whole western coast of England and Scotland, and indeed almost the whole of Ireland, is at this moment unguarded either by ships of war or troops, except a few sloops or cutters to watch smugglers.

We submit to the Congress the following plan: To send three frigates, loaded with tobacco for Nantes or Bordeaux, and that they be manned and commanded in the best possible manner. That on their arrival in either of the above rivers, they make but little appearance of strength, and endeavor to pass for common cruisers; while they are refitting, which should be in different ports, near each other, intelligence might be had of the position of the British fleet, and the circumstances of the different towns on the sea-coast, and of the merchant ships in them; in consequence of which a blow might be struck that would alarm and shake Great Britain, and its credit, to the center. The thought may appear bold and extravagant, yet we have seen as extraordinary events within these two years past, as that of carrying the war to our enemy's doors. As it appears extravagant, it will be in consequence unexpected by them, and the more easily executed. The burning or plundering of Liverpool or Glasgow would do us more essential service than a million of treasure and much blood spent on the continent. It would raise our reputation to the highest pitch, and lessen in the same degree that of our enemy's. We are confident it is practicable, and with very little danger, but times may alter with the arrival of the frigates, yet in that case their cruise on this coast bids fairer to be profitable than on any other, and they may at least carry back in safety many of the stores wanted, which is a most capital object, should the other be laid aside.

Every day's experience confirms to us what is pointed out indeed by nature itself, the necessity of rendering America independent in every sense of the word. The present glorious, though trying contest, will do more to render this independence fixed and certain, if circumstances are seasonably improved, than would otherways have been effected in an age. The manufacturing of any one necessary article among ourselves is like breaking one link of the chains which have heretofore bound the two worlds together, and which our artful enemies had, under the mask of friendship, been long winding round and round us, and binding fast. Thus, as founderies for cannon, iron as well as brass, are erecting, if they are at once erected large enough to cast of any size, we may in future be easy on that important article, and independent on the caprice or interest of our pretended friends for a supply; and to forward this we shall take the liberty of sending over some of the most skillful founders we can meet with.

The jealousy which reigns among the maritime powers of Europe with their narrow, weak, and contemptible system of politics, prevents our being able to procure ships of war, to remedy which you have with you timber, iron, and workmen, and we must send you over sail-cloth and cordage as fast as we can. The importance of having a considerable naval force is too obvious to need our saying more than that we conceive no apparent difficulty or obstruction ought to deter us from pushing it forward to the utmost of our power. We have sent you, by a former conveyance, a plan of a frigate on a new construction, and now send you the duplicate, which we submit to the judgment of those better skilled than we pretend to be in naval affairs, but imagine that on our coast and, perhaps, any where, ships constructed in some such manner may be as formidable as those of seventy-four guns, and it is certain they will cost us less. The vessel building in Amsterdam[1] is on this plan, which we hope will be in season for service this fall or autumn.

We are, with the utmost respect, etc.,

B. Franklin.
S. Deane.

[1] The Indien, of 44 guns, but owing to international complications she was sold to the King of France, who later turned her over to the Chevalier Luxembourg, by whom she was leased in 1779 or 1780 to the State of South Carolina.

[GEORGE CHALMERS TO GEORGE CARLTING[1]]

(Extract)   26 May 1777

I did not return from my little excursion until late on Saturday night & therefore have been as yet able to make no further progress in our business. little of any consequence has occurred since I left there—*Franklin and Dean have been several days in Possession of an Order for the discharge of the seamen at Dunkirk;* but as *they are thought too useful to be lost or allowed to separate, no use has as yet been made of it & consequently they are will be left in their present state until other employment is prepared, in order that they may thus be kept together—I think they will be used in another Privateer.*

Memoranda of Some of Lord Stormont's Correspondence[2]

28 May 1777 Lord Stormont to Lord Weymouth No. 94:—That he expressed to Vergennes His Majesty's satisfaction at the speedy justice done in the restitution of Cunningham's prizes he mentioned at the same time a project now in agitation at Dunkirk for arming two cutters to be commissioned by Franklin and Deane, upon which Vergennes desired that Mr. Frazer should write and inform the Commandant at Dunkirk.

[1] Stevens's Facsimiles, Vol. V, No. 473–1.
[2] *Ibid.,* Vol. XV, No. 1544–10.

[COMTE DE VERGENNES TO THE MARQUIS
DE NOAILLES[1] [2]]

(Extract—Translation)

Explanation of what took place in connection with Mr. Cunningham an American commander of a privateer who brought into Dunkirk two English packet boats which he had seized.

Principles which guided our conduct.

Versailles, 31st. May 1777.

I have received, Sir, the despatch No. 42, which you did me the honour of writing to me on the 23rd of this month.

We are not astonished, Sir, at the diversity of opinions respecting our conduct with regard to Mr. Cunningham; each one judges it according to his personal feelings, or according to how the facts are reported, and I see that they are reported very inexactly: I am going to transmit them to you as they are stated in the *procès-verbaux* on which His Majesty has given his decision.

An English cutter came into the port of Dunkirk; it cleared there with goods for North Faro. A certain Beach was its captain, and it was under his name that the Admiralty permit was granted. Having reached the roadstead, a certain Cunningham, who had secretly collected some sailors, and who, it is said, was furnished with a commission by Congress, got on board this vessel, must have taken command of it, and, under cover of the American flag which he substituted for the English one, ventured to make the captures which he was stupid

[1] The French Ambassador at the Court of St. James.
[2] Stevens's Facsimiles, Vol. XV, No. 1543–1, 3.

enough to bring into Dunkirk. Nothing, assuredly, Sir, is more contrary to the rules of the sea, and to the received usages amongst all nations, and even if the case had not been provided for in the Treaty of Utrecht, the King's justice would not the less have urged His Majesty to give entire satisfaction in the matter to the Court of London: indeed, a neutral nation cannot and ought not to allow armaments in her country, much less those which have such a special stamp of irregularity. There is a great distinction to be drawn between simply admitting, in case of need, and for the moment, a privateer with her prize, and permitting that same privateer to lie, so to speak, in ambush in a neutral port: this latter case is precisely that of Mr. Cunningham; it is therefore, manifest that he could not be regarded as a mere corsair, that he has infringed the laws of the sea, and that he has consequently deserved the treatment which he has experienced, whatever may have been the commission with which he was furnished by Congress. The King owed it to himself to act with rigour on this occasion, and it matters little to His Majesty whether his determination has or has not excited the gratitude of the English. His Majesty in acting as he has done, had no other aim than that of giving to the Court of London a public proof of his justice, of his fidelity in observing treaties, and a striking example of the consideration which nations mutually owe one another. This, Sir, is what we have to answer to the English observers who criticise our conduct.

[THE AMERICAN COMMISSIONERS TO THE COMMITTEE
OF FOREIGN AFFAIRS[1]]

(Extract)   Paris May 28 1777

Agreeable to what we mentioned in ours of the 14
march & 9 apl. (a third Copy of which we send herewith) Mr. Lee tarryed here some weeks after his return
from Spain. No news arriving (tho' we received Letters from you) of any Commissnr. being actually appointed for Prussia, and the necessity for a good understanding with that Court in order to obtain specially a
port in the Northern Seas, appearing more and more
every day on various occasions, he concluded with our
approbation to set out for Berlin which he did a bout a
week since, and we have reason to hope good effects
from that Journey. The points probably in view are
(besides the acknowledgment of american Independency) an open port for German commerce & the permission for fitting out armed Vessels to annoy the
Enemys Northern Trade & disposing of our Prizes. If
those points can be obtained, we are assured we might
soon have a formidable squadron there, & accumulate
seamen to a great amount. The want of such a free port
appears in the late Instance of Mr. Cunningham's arrest in Dunkirk with the Prizes he bro't in: for tho' the
fitting out may be Covered & Concealed by various pretences so as at least to be winked at by Gov't here,
because those pretences afford a good Excuse for not

1 Stevens's Facsimiles, Vol. XV, No. 1541–1.

preventing it, yet the bringing of prizes by a vessel so fitted out, is so Notorious an act and so Contrary to treaties, that if suffered must occasion an immediate war. Cunningham will however thro' favor be discharged with His Vessels we are given to understand, but we must put up with the loss of the prizes, which being reclaimed will be restored. This is an occasion of triumph to our Enemies which we must suffer them to enjoy for the present, assured as we are by the most substantial proof of the Friendship of this Court & of Spain.

[EXTRACT FROM A LETTER FROM SILAS DEANE TO CONRAD A. GERARD[1]]

[Paris, June 2d, 1777]

With respect to the Cutter at Dunkirk, I mean that last purchased,[2] in which individuals are interested, I can only say that I advised my Freinds to get her away as quick & as silently as possible, & to stand directly of the Coast, & on no Consideration permit her to return to France or near Any of its Ports. If I shall be instructed to give better advice, I shall most readily do it, & I doubt not my advice will be attended to, but the Owners have already expended Two Thousand pounds Sterling in the purchase and repairs, which they cannot afford to loose. I hoped farther that Capt. Cunningham & his

---

[1] In The Deane Papers, Collections of the New-York Historical Society, Vol. II, p. 62.　　　　[2] The Revenge.

People might get a passage in her to their Own Country, where they might be useful. I hope at least they may be dismissed from Prison, & be permitted to depart in such manner as they can, though if they disperse, there will be danger of their not returning, & consequently of Our loosing a number of brave and honest Subjects. I can only add, that I am ready to follow most exactly the advice which shall be given me on this & every other Occasion by his Excellency, but am at an uncertainty what to do untill more explicitly informed.

[COMTE DE VERGENNES TO THE MARQUIS DE NOAILLES[1]]

(Extract—Translation)

Paris, June 4th. 1777

Motives which decided the restitution of the Harwich packet, brought into Dunkirk by Captain Cunningham an American.

With regard to Captain Cunningham's adventure, the account which I gave you in my preceeding despatch, will have enabled you to judge, Sir, of the principles and motives which have directed our conduct on this occasion. We were well persuaded in advance that it would not excite the English to gratitude; nor was it for love of them,—but only to do homage to the principles of justice and equity which direct his actions, that His Majesty acted with severity towards the American corsair. Moreover, Sir, Lord Weymouth must know the Treaty of Utrecht imper-

---

[1] Stevens's Facsimiles, Vol. XVI, No. 1546–3.

fectly, if he confounds the affair of Captain Cunningham with that of the frigate Reprisal. If that Minister will give himself the trouble to read this Treaty
again, he will find there the two cases well distinguished, as you have pointed out to him.

[GEORGE LUPTON TO WILLIAM EDEN[1]]

(Extract)

4 June 1777.

Hodge, the fellow that fitted out Conyngham Vessell
is return'd to Dunkirk, from some port near that place
he means to fit out a Vessell and proceed for America
—New port I think will be the place, therefore it
will be necessary to keep a sharp lookout,— . . .
Their is a Capt: Bell here who I mention'd in one of
my former letters, he sets out this Evening for Mar-
seillie, at which port or some other near that place, is
a ship purchased for him. She Carries 20—twelve
pounders on one deck, he is intended to Cruize in the
Mediterranean to intercept some of your homeward
bound Italian Ship loaded with silks, which at this time
of the year is very rich—She is the property of Conyngham & Nesbit, Witting & Morris[2] of Phi"a. & Mr.
Deane of this place, he has a proper Commission, and
everything suitable, the Ship intended for him Sails
very fast, she is called the Sartar, will Carry two hundred men, mostly frenchmen, he has a Credit from
Thos. Morris of Nantes on Stephen Cathalan of Mar-
seilie for what money he may want.

[1] Stevens's Facsimiles, Vol. II, No. 168–3.   [2] Robert Morris.

Extract of a Letter from Guernsey, June 5[1]

An American privateer of twelve guns came into this road yesterday morning; tacked about on the firing of the guns from the Castle, and just off the Island took a large brig bound for this port, which they have since carried into Cherburgh.[2] She had the impudence to send her boat in the dusk of the evening to a little island off here, called Jetto, and unluckily carried off the Lieutenant of Northey's Independent Company here, with the garrison Adjutant, who were shooting rabbits for their diversion. Two gentlemen of consequence are gone to Cherburgh to demand them. The poor pilferers got nothing but six or seven little Guinea pigs made into a pye for the gentlemen's dinner, and a few bottles of claret, though the brig they took is valued at 7000*l.* belonging to 'Squire Tupper.

[1] In the Remembrancer, London, J. Almon, 1777, p. 143.
[2] Cherbourg, France.

[COMTE DE VERGENNES TO THE MARQUIS
DE NOAILLES[1]]

(Translation—Extract)

Versailles, 7th. June 1777

Motives which de-
cided the restitution
of the Harwich
packet, brought into
Dunkirk by Captain
Cunningham, an
American.

With regard to Captain Cunningham's adventure, the account which
I gave you in my preceding despatch,
will have enabled you to judge, Sir,
of the principles and motives which
have directed our conduct on this occasion. We were well persuaded in advance that it
would not excite the English to gratitude; nor was it for
love of them, but only to do homage to the principles of
justice and equity which direct all his actions, that His
Majesty acted with severity towards the American corsair. Moreover, Sir, Lord Weymouth must know the
treaty of Utrecht imperfectly, if he confounds the affair
of Captain Cunningham with that of the frigate Re-

Praise of the reflec-
tions of M. de
Noailles on the help
furnished by our
commerce to the
insurgents.

prisal. If that Minister will give
himself the trouble to read the treaty
again, he will find there the two cases
well distinguished, as you have
pointed out to him. I abstain from
speaking of the reproaches cast on us
with regard to the help which our commerce furnishes
to the insurgents, because there is nothing to add to the
reflections which you have made on the subject to Lord
Weymouth.

[1] Stevens's Facsimiles, Vol. XVI, No. 1546.

Een Engelsche Paket-boot door een Americaanfche Kaaper genoomen
den 2 May A.° 1777.
S. Fokke simonsz Excudit.

The Capture of the Harwich Packet

Extract from the Remembrancer[1]

The Prince of Orange packet, mentioned in the list of vessels taken, was carried into Dunkirk. The smugglers at Dunkirk were exceedingly offended with the bringing the packet into that port. They said it would occasion some English frigate, or armed vessels, to be stationed off that port, which would greatly obstruct their trade; and a desperate quarrel ensued between them and the crew of the American privateer, which had taken and brought in the packet. Upon this, the Commandant at Dunkirk put them all in prison, together with Cunningham, the Captain of the privateer. As soon as advice of the capture reached London, Lord Stormont, the English minister at Paris, presented to the French ministry a memorial, in which he affirmed that the pretended privateer was no other than a pirate, and requested upon that ground the restoration of the prize. Cunningham being in confinement, no answer was immediately given. The privateer had been fitted out at Dunkirk, but it was not known for what purpose; which, and some other irregularities in Cunningham's conduct, were supposed to be the cause of complying with the ambassador's request. However, upon nicer and further examination, the French court were so well satisfied, that Cunningham and his crew were in a short time after released from their confinement.

BRUSSELS, June 9. We are well informed that Mr. Cunningham, Captain of the American privateer the Surprise, sent the mail (with the letters from London of the 29th. of April last) which he took in the Prince of Orange Packet, to Dr. Franklin at Paris.

[1] 1777, p. 146.

*Extract of a Letter from the Postmaster at Harwich,
June 14, to the Postmaster-General at London*

The master of a fishing-smack, arrived here last night
from Dunkirk, acquaints me, that he saw Cunningham
and his crew at large on Thursday last, and they were
proving carriage guns, in order to be put on board a
large cutter[1] of 130 tons; that she was to be navigated
by French sailors to Havre, and that Cunningham and
the crew were going over land, in order to fit her for
sea. He also declared, that he saw a brig in Dunkirk
road, that had got on board the powder, small arms,
ammunition, etc. for the said cutter, which is painted
blue and yellow, which was built for the smuggling
trade, and reported to be a fast sailer; that Cunningham
told him the guns proving were for his use on board the
said vessel; that he said he would soon have another
Harwich boat, which he did not in the least fear but he
should make a legal prize, which also was confirmed by
the crew the same evening at a publick house. I
thought proper to give you this intelligence, and make
no doubt of necessary steps being taken to put a stop to
the proceedings of this daring pirate. She is to mount
20 carriage guns, and to have 50 or 60 men.

I am, Sir, your's,

JAMES CLEMENTS.

(*This letter was sent to Lloyd's Coffee-House by* A.
Todd, *Esq. Secretary to the Post-Master General.*)

[1] The Revenge.

[LORD STORMONT TO LORD WEYMOUTH[1]]
(Extract)

My Lord,   Paris 11 June 1777.

I lost no time in executing the important Orders transmitted to me in your Lordship's Letter No. 38, which I received yesterday Morning. I executed them in the following Manner. By way of Introduction, I mentioned to M. de Vergennes, the Information Mr. Frazer had at my Desire given the Commandant at Dunkirk with regard to the Cutter arming there, and added, that I knew the Commandant by means of this Information, and that, which he himself had collected was apprized of every Particular, and had made his Report accordingly, yet notwithstanding all this Sir, the Armament of this Cutter goes on and will continue, till positive Orders are sent from hence to stop it. He threw in a Word or two about our Smugglers arming more than they used to do for fear of our Cruizers, I told him that this Cutter which was to mount 18 guns at least, was certainly not to be employed as a Smuggling Vessel, but was to carry a Commission from the Congress a Commission that would be issued by Franklin and Deane. This, Sir, is agreeable to a most extraordinary Plan which they have formed, and of which I have more than once given you some Information. They purchase or hire Vessels, which they arm in your Ports, man them with French Sailors, transmit them Commissions from hence and then mean to pass them for American Vessels and send them out as such to Cruize against us. This is the Case of the Cutter at Dunkirk.

[1] Stevens's Facsimiles, Vol. XVI, No. 1548–1, 2.

[SILAS DEANE[1]]

(Note in the third person, unaddressed)

(Extract) *14 Juin 1777.*

Mr. Deane has received Letters from Dunkirk informing that Capt. Cunningham & his Sailors were still detained in prison, & that on the 10th. instant no Orders were received for their discharge, & that some of them' were suffering in their health. Mr. Deane prays that Orders may (if not already sent) be given for their being discharged.

[LORD STORMONT TO LORD WEYMOUTH[2]]

(Extract) *Private*

Paris June 19. 1777.

The order for the release of Cunningham and the other Pirates was granted on the Sollicitation of Franklin and Deane They kept the order for some time without making use of it, being apprehensive that the crew would disperse if they were released before another Ship was ready to receive them. They are now I believe on board the Cutter called the Greyhound that Cutter which I have so often mentioned to M. de Vergennes notwithstanding all my Remonstrances She is to sail in a few days, but has positive orders to return no more to Dunkirk.

[1] Stevens's Facsimiles, Vol. III, No. 700–1.
[2] *Ibid.,* Vol. XVI, No. 1552–3.

[LORD STORMONT TO LORD WEYMOUTH[1]]

(Extract)   Paris June 25th. 1777

I then, My Lord resumed my Discourse, and told Him[2] that I would begin with what was doing at our very Doors, and mentioned the Particulars relating to the Greyhound cutter as they are stated in Your Lordships Letter. I added with Truth, that these facts are so Notorious, so Public, that they are mentioned in Letters to foreign ministers here who have no direct Interest in the Matter, and were talked of at our last Sundays Assembly. He answered that it had not been found upon examination that the Cutter was armed, I replied that she certainly had her Guns on board, and that those Guns had been purchased in France, that whether she had them mounted or not was a Matter of indifference, she was equally to be considered as a Vessel that had arrived in a french Port which was a thing He must admit to be contrary to all Rules. He went to his Table to take down in writing the Name of *Hodge,* I desired Him likewise to note that Cunningham and the other Pirates were to go on board this Ship, and were publicly employed in equipping Her, and proving Her Cannon etc, I observed to Him, how highly aggravating this circumstance was, and said that it was very singular indeed, that Pirates who were imprisoned and ought to have been tried and punished as such, should not only

---

[1] Stevens's Facsimiles, Vol. XVI, No. 1556–7, 8.
[2] M. de Maurepas.

be released but allowed to embark again in the same Port, and for the self same Purpose. I told him that Cunningham was to command this Cutter, and Has said that all that was enjoyned Him was not to return to Dunkirk; I ended what I had to say on this subject with observing, that in this Case no want of Information could be alleged, as Mr. Frazer had in consequence of my Letter written at His Excellencies desire, given the Commander at Dunkirk all the particulars, and that Commander had made an ample Report.

Extract of a Letter from Dunkirk, June 26[1]

This morning, between eight and nine o'clock, Capt. Cunningham and Capt. Roberts sailed from this place in two ships, built, armed, and manned here; these ships belong to some person in M. de S——'s[2] favour, and are to cruise against the English and Portuguese ships, chiefly, as it is represented, against the mails: Cunningham pledged his honour to his employers on sailing, that they should hear from him; the ship on board which he is, is one of the best sailers known; the crew is composed of all the most desperate fellows which could be procured in so blessed a port as Dunkirk.

[1] In the Remembrancer, 1777, p. 173. [2] Sartine.

[PAUL WENTWORTH TO THE EARL OF SUFFOLK[1]]

(Extract)

29 June 1777

I am well informed, that Cunningham & his Crew are at large at Dunkirk, & that the surprise Privateer, was restored to him; & is ready to go, if not gone by this time, to sea as a Privateer. Mr. DeSartine sent a Commissary of Marines to Cherbourg to acquire & make a recital in form of the Circumstances attending the Capture of Capt. Burnell & his Lieutenant, by the Capt. of the Cutter etc. etc.—which Your Lordship has heard of some time ago—It is presumed this affair will be the subject of a Complaint.

[WILLIAM CARMICHAEL TO THE AMERICAN
COMMISSIONERS[2]]

Gentlemen,—

I arrived here this morning with a determination to comply with your orders & not to suffer Captn. Cunningham to sail but as a merchant vessel returning with merchantable property to his own country. I found the parties concernd Disposd, of themselves, to comply with this disposition, heartily sick of having ever attempted

[1] Stevens's Facsimiles, Vol. II, No. 175–1.
[2] In The Deane Papers, Collections of the New-York Historical Society, Vol. II, p. 85.

other projects & resolved for the future to seek other scenes of action, where they might more effectually serve themselves & Country. From doing this they are prevented by an order from Court, which disables them from sailing unless they give security not only that they shall not make prizes in the present voyage, tho' they should do it in consequence of being attackd by the Enemy, but such is the tenor of the order (as I am informd) that the security will be liable to be calld upon in case even after the arrival of their paltry little vessel in America any other Person should purchase it for a privateer. Strangers unknown, & as it seems in the Eyes of the inhabitants here, unprotected, can never hope to find security against such remote consequences. So that unless Administration grants these unfortunate sufferers the same privilege that is taken every day by our Enemies in this port, they must give up the property imbarked in the adventure & return, each one execrating french timidity, partiality and politics, to his own Country, or seek happier fortune in the shore opposite to this. To sell their vessel will be impossible, as no one will venture to buy a vessel so circumstanc'd, & their goods that make up the Cargo will inevitably be disposd of to vast loss. I beg you to represent this in a proper place & manner. The Manifest, spoken of, would have been sent up in a few days, had not this unexpected order arrivd, & you would have heard no more on a subject that has given you, Gentlemen, so much uneasiness & has so much exposd us in the eyes of the world. Our Countrymen that escape from Captivity in England fly to this place as an asylum. Could they be incouraged here we should soon have not only many of them, but many English sailors who fly from the Press

or desert the service, & from hence we could send them
to other ports less offensive to England. I shall do myself the honor to write you more fully next post. I am,
Gentlemen, Your most obedt humble Sert.,

Dunkerque, June 30th, 1777. WM. CARMICHAEL.

[M. DE GUICHARD[1] TO THE COMTE DE VERGENNES[2]]

(Translation)

M. de Rayneval[3]   Dunkirk. 1st. July 1777
Answered 7th. July

Monseigneur

Representation of Mr. Hodge as to the detention of his smuggling vessel at Dunkirk.

I have the honour to report to you, agreeably to your
letter of the 31st. May last, in which you expressed to
me your desire to be informed of the events which take
place in the port and road of Dunkirk. In consequence,
I have the honour to inform you, Monseigneur, that
Mr. Hodge, owner of a smuggling vessel, intended for
the coast of Ireland, has just told me that, in accordance
with orders from the Court, his vessel could not be dis-
patched unless he gave security that he would not go
pirating against the English. Mr. Hodge, being an
American, is perhaps suspected of wishing to give another destination to his vessel when he is out at sea; he is
asked for security,—an unknown stranger would find

[1] The commandant at Dunkirk.
[2] Stevens's Facsimiles, Vol. XVI, No. 1560–1.
[3] Gérard de Rayneval, later Minister Plenipotentiary to the Continental Congress and Consul-General of France in America.

nobody to answer for him. Mr. Hodge also added that, without mention of security, permission had been given him, some days ago to leave port to carry on smuggling, which decided him to put goods on board his ship and raise a crew which costs him 250 livres a day. He says that by requiring him to give security he is reduced to selling his vessel and goods at a loss, and to pay his crew for the campaign, which puts him in danger of being reduced to beggary. I must not hide from you, Monseigneur, that this American is in despair. Probably Captain Cunningham, who has been given his liberty and his vessel, will be treated like Mr. Hodge.

I am with very profound respect,
Monseigneur
Your very humble and
very obedient servant
DE GUICHARD.

Extract from the Remembrancer[1]

LONDON, July 4. The following advertisement appeared in all the daily news-papers:

"New Lloyd's Coffee-house,
"July 3, 1777.

"THE merchants, owners of ships, and insurers, observing that the French, in violation of the laws of nations, have permitted American privateers not only to bring in British ships and cargoes, but also to sell the same in their ports in Europe and the West-Indies, many of which privateers, it is well known are the property of, and manned by, Frenchmen; and whereas a continuance of such practice must prove ruinous to the

[1] London, 1777, p. 176.

commercial interests of this kingdom, the owners of all such ships and cargoes as have been, or may be, taken, and sold in any of the ports of France or the West-Indies, are earnestly intreated to send the particulars thereof to Lord Viscount Weymouth, his Majesty's Secretary of State for the southern department, and also to the Lords of the Admiralty, in order that Administration may be fully apprised of the alarming extent of this growing and destructive evil."

For the Remembrancer

The number of our ships taken by the American and French privateers is truly alarming; and what appears more surprising is, that We scarcely ever hear of any of those privateers being taken, but frequently a number of their trading ships.—This circumstance, to the intelligent English merchant, accounts for the mystery, viz. in former wars the first object of administration was, to protect our own commerce, then to annoy the enemy's; for which purpose, besides the proper convoys, a number of our men of war were ordered to cruze in the various tracts and latitudes of OUR TRADE, which effectually secured it. The residue of our fleet was either employed in squadrons against the enemy, or in single ships in the latitudes of THEIR TRADE, to destroy it. But this wise and safe system has been reversed, for the sake of encouraging a few naval commanders, at the expence of the merchants; for our officers are now at liberty, without any regard to the protection of our trade, to cruize in the latitudes of the enemy's, where they joyfully succeed in taking some prizes.

[M. DE GUICHARD TO THE COMTE DE VERGENNES[1]]

(Translation)

Dunkirk, 7th. July 1777

M. de Rayneval
answered 15 July

Monseigneur

Sale by Mr. Hodge, an American, of his vessel to an Irishman, to carry on smuggling on the coasts of England.

I have the honour to inform you that I was asked yesterday by the officers of the Admiralty to give assistance to their guards. I annex to my letter a copy of their requisition. I think Mr. Hodge is in question, the American who sold the vessel, very well armed, to an Irishman, doubtless to carry on smuggling on the coasts of England. For some time past all the smugglers have been so armed. It appears also that the Admiralty fears that this vessel may depart without clearance; it is at present in the middle of the Channel, at a good gunshot from our entrenchments. I have given orders to all the guard-stations of the port and to those in the neighbourhood to give help to the Admiralty's guards, conformably to the requisition which has been made to me. As there is no cannon to defend the channel, nor any chain, I think that an armed vessel can easily leave it, or enter

[1] Stevens's Facsimiles, Vol. XVI, No. 1564–1.

it with a favourable wind, without anyone being able to oppose it: it is a matter of four minutes.

I am with very profound respect,

Monseigneur,

Your very humble and very obedient servant

DE GUICHARD.

P.S. A snow[1] belonging to the King of England anchored in this roadstead at three o'clock this afternoon, it is said to be armed with 14 guns.[2] The English who are in Dunkirk instruct their compatriots well.

Mr. Richard Allen, the new proprietor of the vessel on account of which the Admiralty had asked my assistance, has been of his own accord to the Quay Master to ask permission to bring his vessel in again and place it opposite the guard-house of the port, where he is at present unloading his powder.

[LORD STORMONT TO LORD WEYMOUTH[3]]

(Extract)   *Separate and Secret.*

Paris July 9th. 1777.

I went next My Lord to what is doing at Dunkirk, and told M de Vergennes that it was certain that there was an Intention of sending Military Stores and Artillery from thence to North America, that that was the

---

[1] A vessel equipped with two masts, resembling the main and foremasts of a ship, and a third small mast just abaft the mainmast, carrying a sail nearly similar to a ship's mizzen, called a trysail.

[2] The Speedwell, commanded by Captain Harvey. See p. 62.

[3] Stevens's Facsimiles, Vol. XVI, No. 1568–3.

object of Beaumarchais[1] Secretary's Journey to Dunkirk, that Carmichael not finding him I suppose expe-
ditious enough, was gone to quicken His Diligence, that
that cutter I had so repeatedly mentioned to His Excellency was going to sail, tho' Hodge himself had owned
to the *Commandant de la Marine* that she belonged to
Him and it was notorious to every body that she was
Armed in the Port of Dunkirk. I added that according to my last Information there is a very Extraordinary
Project with regard to Her; French sailors are to Navi-
gate Her to Bordeaux or Nantes, and Cunningham and
the rest of the crew are to go by land. M de Vergennes
said, that that will not be, and added that his opinion
was that the cutter should be sold in the Port of Dunkirk.

[GEORGE LUPTON TO WILLIAM EDEN[2]]

(Extract)

9 July 1777.

In my last I mentioned that Carmichael was gone to
Dunkirk, by the last Accounts he was there still assisting
Capt. Conyngham to despatch his old Vessell, and making provision for a 20 Gun Ship which they mean to
send from the same or some neighbouring port.

[1] Caron de Beaumarchais, an enthusiast in the American cause, who
greatly influenced French policy at this time. The aid advanced to
the struggling colonies by the French government was sent through
him, and, to make these transactions still more secret, through a
fictitious mercantile house, under the name of Hortalez & Co. Over
a million francs from the French government and another million
from Spain were thus forwarded to America in the summer of 1776
alone by Beaumarchais.

[2] Stevens's Facsimiles, Vol. II, No. 179–3.

[WILLIAM CARMICHAEL TO THE AMERICAN
COMMISSIONERS[1]]

Gentlemen,—   Dunkerque, July 10th, 1777.

I have had the honor of receiving your Letter of the
7th of July, and am sorry that you have not had an opportunity of yet applying to the Minister on the subject
of Mr. Hodge's vessel. The bond required was to give
security here that the vessel should not cruise against
the English. The expressions of the Minister's letters
were so vague and general, that the officers here were
obliged to write up to court for an explanation of the
Minister's intentions; so that untill answers to those letters arrive, things must remain in STATU QUO, to the
great cost & risque of the owner. I wrote you that five
English cruisers are now employed to watch her motions, three of which are in this road. Were it not that
it will be disagreeable, probably, to the Court of France
to have its Ports thus blocked up, I would advise you to
buy this vessel from the owner, & apply it merely to the
purpose of giving business to the English Commissary
here & of detaining so many English vessels in the
neighbourhood of this Port, instead of cruizing against
our trade. At all events, an individual cannot afford to
be at the expence, so that if orders should not be ex-
pedited before this reaches you, I must again repeat our
request that you would pray the Ministry to be so explicit in their orders that nothing may create longer

[1] In The Deane Papers, Collections of the New-York Historical
Society, Vol. II, p. 89.

delay. Mr. Hodge will be obliged again to take back his property, as he sold her without informing the owner of the peculiarity of her situation. As you expressed a desire to have a copy of the Letter wrote by the Compte De Maurepas to Parker Forth, (1) I have been at some pains to obtain the general purport of it, which translated is as follows:

"Sir,—I am not surprized that the effect of his Lordship's illness and the variety of business in which he is involved should plead as his excuse for not writing. The capture of the Packett boat (2) must, I dare say, have made a great noise with you. The affair is very simple; the vessel which took her was cleard out as a smuggler. Not one of the crew were French. The manner of clearance & the precautions taken with respect to the crew will acct for the secrecy with which the plan was carried on. Every method hath been taken to come at the bottom of the affair and to procure the necessary reparation. The Paquet shall be restord; the desire of continuing the peace cannot be expressed by his Lordship with more fervor than it is wishd by me. I shall always think myself happy to display these sentiments as well as the regard with which I am, etc. etc.

"M—— [MAUREPAS]."

As you know the manner in which I obtained this, & that it is often impossible to have opportunity to copy, altho' one may have time to read such things, the not being able to produce the original or literal copy is a circumstance of no great moment. If you think it is of any consequence, I can obtain you the history of this man's intrigues, by which, at least, the French Minister may see what a low lifd criminal they honor with their notice. I have been very unwell since my arrival, but hope a change of weather will recruit me. The Merchants here are alarmd at the Captures made by the English. If the Ministry would communicate to the Chamber of Commerce their intentions of reclaiming their vessels and of protecting their trade, it would remove their apprehensions and increase the number of adventurers to our part of the world. Mr. Hodge is obliged to apply to you for a credit, as his expedition has been attended with such additional expence, occasioned by the delay, that he tells me his funds are quite exhausted. I beg my Compliments to Dr. Bancroft & Mr Franklin, & am, Gentlemen, your most obedt humble Sert.

WM. CARMICHAEL.

The Lugger[1] is made French property, & is ready to be sent round to Nantes whenever Mr Hodge shall receive your orders.

Since writing the preceeding I find that we shall have no farther delay in getting out this vessel, which we shall set out with as much expedition as possible.

To the honorble Benjamin Franklin &
Silas Deane, Esqrs, at Paris.

[1] The Surprize was sold to Dominique Morel, a French widow.

[M. DE GUICHÀRD TO THE COMTE DE VERGENNES[1]]

(Translation)

Dunkirk 11th. July 1777.

M. de Rayneval

answered 16th. July

Monseigneur

Order held by Mr. Harvey commanding an English snow to burn even in the
Dunkirk Road every American vessel.

I have the honour to inform you that M. de Villers,
Naval Commissary, had just told me, before M D'Hersin, Lieutenant General of the Admiralty, that Mr.
Frazer had just informed him that the snow Speedwell, commanded by Captain Harvey,[2] which had
been at anchor at the entrance of the harbour since the
7th. instant, had orders to remain in the road to await
the departure of the vessel which Mr. Hodge has sold
to an Irishman and which is fitted out as a smuggler, to
burn it wherever he might find it, were it even in the
road. I have the honour, Monseigneur, to annex to my
letter copy of one from the Duc de Choiseul, which does
not agree with [qy. disapproves of] a similar act of
violence. As we have neither boom nor guns to defend
the port, the channel nor the road, Mr. Harvey can
easily carry out his orders. Mr. Frazer also told M. de
Villers that that officer did not intend to molest any
other vessels leaving the port, but the American Mr.
Hodge declared this morning to M. D'Hersin in the

---

[1] Stevens's Facsimiles, Vol. XVI, No. 1569–1.   [2] See p. 57.

presence of M. de Villers that several merchant vessels from the United Colonies were expected here, which will arrive immediately, and will doubtless be captured by Captain Harvey or by other vessels of the King of England, which make their appearance every moment in our road.

> I am with very profound respect
> Monseigneur
> Your very humble and
> very obedient servant
> DE GUICHARD.

[M. DE GUICHARD TO THE COMTE DE VERGENNES[1]]

(Translation)

Dunkirk, 12th. July 1777
12-30 p.m.

M. de Rayneval

received the 15th.
answered 16th. July

Monseigneur

Mr. Frazer declares that Mr. Harvey commanding an English snow, has orders to attack and to burn, even in the roadstead of Dunkirk, all American vessels.

I have the honour to report to you that Mr. Frazer has this morning left my house, accompanied by an officer of the small vessel which is in the roadstead, aside of the snow[2] commanded by Mr. Harvey. Mr. Frazer confirmed to me all that I had the honour of reporting to you yesterday, assuring me that Mr. Harvey had orders from his Court to attack every American, or vessels sus-

[1] Stevens's Facsimiles, Vol. XVI, No. 1570.
[2] The Speedwell. See pp. 57 and 62.

pected to be such, and to destroy them without distinction of place. Mr. Frazer told me that he thought it his duty to communicate to the Commandant of the place the order held by Mr. Harvey. I replied to him that this order might appear extraordinary to the French Court. I have had the honour, Monseigneur, to report to you the situation of the port, the channel, and the roadstead; these three objects are absolutely defenceless: I venture to beg you to be good enough to send orders to me as soon as possible concerning the conduct I am to observe; meanwhile, I will do what I can to defend myself against a premeditated insult, in case it should take place, and which is announced to me by Mr. Frazer, the English Commissary.

I am with very profound respect, Monseigneur
Your very humble
and very obedient servant
DE GUICHARD.

[WILLIAM CARMICHAEL TO GUSTAVUS CONYNGHAM[1]]

Captn Cunningham
as with much difficulty the Commissioners of the United States of North America now at Paris, have obtained Liberty for you to sail from Dunkerque, and as it has been on express Condition that you should not cruise against the Commerce of England, I beg & intreat you In the name & by the orders of the Commissioners,

[1] MSS. in the collection of Mr. James Barnes.

that you do nothing which may involve your security or occasion umbrage to the Ministry of France. Notwithstanding which if necessity obliges you to obtain provisions of which your stock is not abundant, on account of the abrupt manner in which you are obliged to leave the Port, or If attackd first by our Enemies, the circumstances of the case will extenuate in favor of your conduct, either in making prizes for your own preservation, or in making reprisal for damages sustaind, Nothing of this sort happening you are to proceed directly to America, Delivering as soon as possible the dispatches intrusted to your Care & taking your further orders from your Employers there. Wishing you success & prosperity I am &c

WM. CARMICHAEL

Dunkerque July 15th. 1777

[LORD STORMONT TO LORD WEYMOUTH[1]]

(Extract)

Paris July 16th. 1777

I spoke fully and strongly to M de Vergennes about the Greyhound Cutter, observed to Him how very Extraordinary it was, that notwithstanding all the circumstances of the case, and all my Repeated Representations, those very Men, who M de Maurepas had formally promised should be tried as Pirates, should not only be set at Liberty, but allowed to equip and arm a Vessel in the self same Port, with an avowed intention

---

[1] Stevens's Facsimiles, Vol. XVI, No. 1575-6.

of cruizing against us, and should be suffered actually to put to sea, which I knew was the case, for tho' an accident had prevented the ship getting out of the Harbour, she certainly was under sail; I added, that it was now Notorious that she had ammunition, as she had unloaded a very considerable Quantity of Gunpowder. (M de Vergennes said that she had been forced to unload it) He added that it now appeared that she was not the property of Hodge, but was publicly claimed by an Englishman (one Richards if I remember right,) He admitted however that this might be a fraud, and concluded with saying, that his advice to M. de Sartines was to end the whole Matter at once by purchasing the Vessel. I told Him in Reply to this, that I knew Cunningham had not relinquished the Project of cruising with this cutter, that He had an Intention of Lying in wait for a Rich West India Man, and that I knew some frenchmen to be on board of Him. (for the sake of my Informer I did not care to say more; the Persons I alluded to are two cadets in the Duke of Fitzjames Regt) M de Vergennes repeated the advice he had given M de Sartines, and I could not but admit that this Expedient would effectually stop Cunninghams Design.

[LORD STORMONT TO LORD WEYMOUTH [1]]

(Extract)   Paris July 16th. 1777

I spoke to him of the two Americans gone to hire
Ships at Nantes—of the constant encouragement Franklin gave to all such Designs, and of the aim he Franklin
had in view; He admitted this, said it was clear that all
this was done in Hopes of forcing a Rupture, that these
insults on our coast, and cruizing against us in Europe,
could have no other View, and was of no sort of consequence *pour décider l'affaire Générale.* He ended
with saying, that this Project should be presented, and
dropped a Word or two about Franklin, that He had
been properly wrote to et *savoit à quoi sen tenir.* I spoke
of the Dunkirk cutter. He assured me she never would
put to sea . . . of the two Ships at Marseilles, and He
repeated what He said last Week, that they were Stopt
and would not go.

Intelligence from a very undoubted authority [2]

Carmichael sent to Dunkirk to join Hodge in fitting
& sending to see [*sic*] a large Cutter mounting 14 Guns,
Commanded by Cunningham & having 70 Men, including the whole Crew of *the Surprize.* One of Cunninghams officers being lately wounded in an affray at
Dunkirk two English Seamen were imprisoned on
suspicion of giving the wound.

[1] Stevens's Facsimiles, Vol. XVI, No. 1575–17.
[2] Enclosure in the letter from Paul Wentworth to the Earl of
Suffolk, 17 July 1777; in Stevens's Facsimiles, Vol. II, No. 182–20.

[M. DE GUICHARD TO THE COMTE DE VERGENNES[1]]

(Translation)

Dunkirk, 20 July 1777.

Monseigneur

Departure from Dunkirk
of the vessel commanded
by Mr. Harvey.
Departure of the smuggling
vessel of the American Mr. Hodge.

I have the honour to acknowledge the receipt of your letter of the 16th. instant. The frigate l'Etourdie has been in our roadstead since the 18th. I do not doubt for a single moment that the English Commissary caused the two vessels of his nation to leave; he may have thought that I should report to the Court the declaration which he made me; he will have judged the time necessary for me to receive a reply, either by post or a courier, and concluded that the two vessels which blocked the port, not being strong enough to resist, it was better to cause them to retire than to expose them.

I should not have failed, Monseigneur, if the occasion had presented itself, to repel force by force, as far as it would have been possible for me to do so without artillery.

The smuggling vessel of Mr. Hodge, who is the owner of it, left on the 17th., at half past nine in the evening in compliance with the intentions of the Court.

[1] Stevens's Facsimiles, Vol. XVI, No. 1582–1.

This smuggler has undergone two examinations, one by the Naval Commissary, and the other by the Admiralty, the vessel being under canvas. No Frenchmen were found upon it. I had this smuggler escorted along both jetties: two or three Englishmen who had remained in town on business returned to the vessel; but, Monseigneur, if, in the country, on the coast, or in the dunes during the night any Frenchman has been hidden, who may have found means of joining the smuggler, that is impossible for me to anticipate or prevent.

The Prince de Robecq did me the honour to write to me on the 18th. that he would sup with me this evening.

I am with very profound respect, Monseigneur,
Your very humble and very obedient servant

DE GUICHARD.

[PAUL WENTWORTH TO THE EARL OF SUFFOLK[1]]

(Extract) 22 July 1777

The pleasure in obeying your lordship's Command, will sometimes induce me, as at present, to trouble you with trivial occurrences. A fisherman boarded Capt. Baggot of the Desborough, as He was carrying us out of Harwich Harbour, to give him caution about Cunningham, who sailed out of Dunkirk Harbour in a Privateer mounting 14 Guns last fryday Evening steering N.E. by N.----

[1] Stevens's Facsimiles, Vol. II, No. 183–1.

Memoranda of Some of Lord Stormont's Correspondence[1]

23 July 1770 Lord Stormont to Lord Weymouth. Most Confidential:—In a conversation with a friend of Lord Stormont's [qy. Mr. Forth], Count de Maurepas expressed his sentiments on the difficulty of his situation surrounded by cabal and intrigue—the disposition of the King is for peace but he is beset by people who endeavour to shake him—the Minister seemed excessively angry at the Greyhound cutter being allowed to go out of Dunkirk and spoke of the conduct of Spain in the dispute with Portugal with some displeasure.

[MARQUIS DE NOAILLES TO THE COMTE DE VERGENNES[2]]

(Extract—Translation)

London, 25th July 1777.

Complaints of Lord Weymouth of the departure of Captain Cunningham from Dunkirk to go privateering.

That we were at present giving assurances which left nothing to be desired, but that all depended now on the execution of the orders which had been sent to our ports, to prevent henceforth the American captains from abusing the refuge which they found with us; and not wishing to express his distrust too clearly relative to the non-execution of these orders, he spoke to me again about Captain Cunningham, who had been released, and had now left Dunkirk to go privateering.

[1] Stevens's Facsimiles, Vol. XVI, No. 1600–7.
[2] *Ibid.,* No. 1587–6.

[LORD WEYMOUTH TO LORD STORMONT[1]]

(Extract)   St. James's 25th July 1777

What has lately happened at Dunkirk does not give great encouragement to believe that a severe execution of the orders sent to the ports will be observed; since Cunningham's vessel has been allowed to sail on security being given by Hodge, who cannot be considered in this case as a responsible man. This circumstance does not agree with the assurances given to Your Excellency by M de Vergennes, and confirmed by M. de Maurepas, and does not imply that good faith on which He values Himself, which the frankness and candour of this Court deserves, and which the present situation requires.

I am to signify to Your Excellency His Majesty's commands, that you acquaint the French Ministers of these particulars; and further inform them, that their professions are agreeable to Him; but that Your Excellency is directed to apprize them of every circumstance that shall come to your knowledge in which the orders which they engage shall be observed shall in naywise have been eluded. In such critical situations a relaxation in the execution would be of the utmost importance.

Your Excellency will endeavour to obtain information what has become of the five prizes taken by the Reprisal and her consorts, and said to have been carried into Nantes. That in case they are still permitted to

---

[1] Stevens's Facsimiles, Vol. XVI, No. 1588–3, 5.

remain in that Port, Your Excellency may claim them for the benefit of the owners.

The sequestration of the three privateers the Reprisal, the Lexington, and Dolphin would be a proper measure if such security will be required of them as shall be of effect; but if such is taken, as has been with respect to Cunningham; it would seem that they are only waiting till a favourable opportunity shall offer to do more injury to this Country.

[LORD STORMONT TO LORD WEYMOUTH[1]]

(Extract)   Paris July 30th. 1777

Notwithstanding the most positive assurances given to me by M. de. Maurepas that the Greyhound Cutter should not sail; a very few Days ago, after that promise was given, which, as was my Duty I mentioned to my Court exactly as it was, that Vessel was publickly suffered to put to sea, and the Admiralty of Dunkirk took Security from Hodge who cannot be considered as a responsible Man in this Case, and I believe is so in None; besides Sir there is a clear contradiction in this whole affair that appears upon the face of it, Richard Allen is allowed to declare the Ship is his Property, and Hodge gives security. If the Property is not for Hodge how can He answer for what the crew will or will not do? If he is the owner how comes Allen to be admitted to make a Declaration that is manifestly false? To

---

[1] Stevens's Facsimiles, Vol. XVI, No. 1591–4.

compleat the whole that Pirate Cunningham is suffered to go on board this Vessel not indeed in the Harbour but in the Road. M de Vergennes seemed uneasy and ashamed whilst I was speaking on the Subject, and when I had done attempted no Justification but said if Cunningham had been suffered to go on board *ses Messieurs de l'Amirauté ne s'en étoient pas vanté* that He did not know that Hodge had given security but understood that the Ship had been suffered to put to sea upon Richard Allen's Declaration that she was his Property. He assured me that the whole was without the approbation of this Court, and had been owing to a Blunder of the *Amirauté* who had thought that after Allen had claimed Her the ship was no longer within the Orders, but was to be treated like any other English Vessel.

[MARQUIS DE NOAILLES TO THE COMTE
DE VERGENNES[1]]

(Extract—Translation)

London, 1st. August 1777

Captures made by Cunningham, one of which was recaptured by the English, and on which nineteen Frenchmen were found.

Continuing to speak with warmth, he[2] related to me a fact of which I had been informed three days before; that the corsair Cunningham had made three captures in the German Ocean, of which one[3] had been recovered and taken into Yarmouth: that the vessel which had been recovered (and which I know had been

[1] Stevens's Facsimiles, Vol. XVI, No. 1592–6. [2] Lord Suffolk.
[3] The Northampton, captured on July 21st. See p. 76.

despatched to Bilboa) had twenty-one men on board, of whom sixteen were Frenchmen. I did not display any surprise at this account, telling him that in a great nation there were many turbulent spirits eager to run after adventures; that in speaking to Lord Weymouth of the latest proofs which we had given of our friendly disposition, conformably to our treaties, I had taken care to warn that Secretary of State that we could not promise to prevent transgressions of private individuals, but only to bring them to justice when they were denounced to us: that, moreover, I did not reclaim the Frenchmen of whom he had just spoken, and that it was enough to declare that they appeared to us to be guilty.

[LORD WEYMOUTH TO LORD STORMONT[1]]

(Extract)   St. James's 1, Augst. 1777

Cunningham's vessel immediately on sailing from Dunkirk has taken several prizes. He had a considerable number of French subjects on board. This fact is clearly ascertained. He put twenty one men on board one of the vessels he had taken; the English have brought this prize[2] into Yarmouth; and on examination it appears that sixteen out of the twenty one men from Cunningham's ship, were French; whose names I inclose with the several papers respecting this report.

The Agents of the American Rebels boast that as the

1 Stevens's Facsimiles, Vol. XVI, No. 1593–1, 2.
2 The Northampton. See pp. 73, 76.

Reprisal was not in a situation to put to sea from the damage sustained in her chase by the Burford, a pretence has been concocted with M. de Sartine that shall allow a sufficient delay to enable her to refit for another cruize; and that the Dolphin is to be continued as a Smuggler, as she was at first; and a frigate bought at St. Malo is to be fitted out to replace Her.

[COMTE DE VERGENNES TO THE MARQUIS DE NOAILLES[1]]

(Extract)   Versailles, 2 August 1777

Explanation on the subject of Captain Cunningham, and the ruse which he made use of to continue privateering on leaving Dunkirk. With regard to Lord Weymouth's reproaches on the subject of Mr. Cunningham, they are ill founded, and prove that this Secretary of State is not served accurately by his spies. There was no legitimate motive to detain that corsair any longer; and if his vessel is again privateering, it is without our knowledge, and only through the interposition of an English subject, named *Richard Allen*. That individual bought at the Admiralty of Dunkirk, from Mr. Hodge, this same vessel, which is a corvette called the Levrier (Greyhound): he obtained from the Admiralty on having made that purchase, permission to leave, on guaranteeing that the said corvette was going to Bergen in Norway for the purpose of trade, and that it was not intended for privateering, a guarantee which was ratified and con-

[1] Stevens's Facsimiles, Vol. XVI, No. 1594-7, 8.

firmed, it is said, by Mr. Hodge. The English Ministry will see, by these details, that we have not favoured, directly or indirectly, the new destination of the vessel in question. Strictly speaking, the Admiralty at Dunkirk might be accused of having been too easy; but the Government has had absolutely no share in the matter, and besides, the English Ministry ought not to impute it to any but one of His Britannic Majesty's own subjects.

[LORD STORMONT TO THE COMTE DE VERGENNES[1]]

(Translation)
                                    Paris, 5th. August 1777.

> Lord Stormont sends a Congress Commission with the list of Frenchmen taken on the vessel Northampton Capt. Cuningham.[2]

Sir

I have the honour to send you herewith the two papers of which I spoke to you this morning. I will not send any remarks with them, being persuaded, Monsieur le Comte, that it is sufficient to submit them to your judgment. I have the honour to be, with perfect attachment,

                    Sir,
                        Your Excellency's very humble
                        and very obedient servant

                                            STORMONT

His Excellency Count de Vergennes.

[1] Stevens's Facsimiles, Vol. XVI, No. 1595.   [2] See p. 73.

[CONGRESS. JOHN HANCOCK, PRESIDENT. COMMIS-
SION TO GUSTAVUS CUNNINGHAM[1]]

(Extract)

avec la lettre de M. Stormount
du 9 août 1777

2 May 1777

In Congress[2]

The Delegates of the united Colonies of new Hamp-
shire, Massachusetts Bay, Rhode Island, Connecticut,
New York, New Jersey, Pensilvania, the counties of
New Castle, Kent and Sussex' on Deleware, Maryland,
Virginia, North Carolina, South Carolina, and
Georgia' To Gustavus Cunningham Greeting.

We reposing special Confidence in your Patriotism,
Valour, Conduct and Fidelity do by these presents constitute and appoint you to be Captain and Commander
of the Armed Vessel or Cutter called the Revenge in
the service of the thirteen united Colonies of North
America, fitted out for the Defence of American Liberty, and repelling every Hostile Invasion thereof. You
are carefully to discharge the Duty of Captain and
Commander by doing and performing all manner of
things thereunto belonging and we do strictly charge
and require all Officers, Marines and seamen under

---

[1] Stevens's Facsimiles, Vol. XVI, No. 1589–1, 2.

[2] This was the new commission issued by the American Commissioners to Conyngham to replace his of March 1, 1777, which was
sent to the Court of Versailles, when he was imprisoned, in May,
1777, and never returned to him.

your command to be obedient to your orders as Commander. And you are to observe and follow such Orders and directions from Time to Time as you shall receive from this or a future Congress of the united Colonies or a Committee of Congress for that Purpose appointed, or Commander in chief for the time being of the Navy of the United Colonies, or any other superior officer according to the Rules and Discipline of War the usage of the sea, and the Instructions herewith given you in pursuance of the Trust reposed in you This commission to remain in Force until revoked by this or a future Congress.

May 2d ⎱
1777 ⎰ Philadelphia

By order of the Congress

JOHN HANCOCK President

Attest

Chars. Thompson Secy
    a True Copy

I do hereby certify that this Congress Commission was delivered to me on board the Revenge cutter by Gustavus Cunningham on the 21st day of July 1777, when appointed Prize Master of the Brig Northampton by the Name of James Smith as Witness my hand in Yarmouth Roads 6th July 1777

BENJ. BAILEY

Witness Jno. Moore.

avec la lettre de M. de Stormont
      du 5 août 1777
Copy.

French seamen on board the Northampton Brig 26 July 1777.

Nicholas Blanché
Pierre Mongoner
Michael Covar
Alexander Tellois
Sanome Bodin
Jean Nicard
Henry Tille
Louis Lecomte

Charel O'Charel
Joseph Nerbal
Battaywz Bodin
François Mulle
François Bzoipi
François Noimielle
Aimable Tillois
Alexander Boll

A List of the English seamen on board The Northampton Brig 26th. July 1777.

Benjm. Bailiy, Alias Smith, Prize Master—an American.

François Mulligan
Joseph Buchannan

James Ashley
Pridman Anderson

[LORD STORMONT TO LORD WEYMOUTH[1]]

(Extract)

My Lord   Paris August 6th 1777.

When I went to M de Vergennes I told Him, that I must beg his particular attention, as what I had to say was by Express order from My Court.

The King my Master, who received with real satisfaction the solemn assurances conveyed, first thro' me, and repeated by the french Ambassador, sees with concern and surprize; that Notwithstanding those assurances, your orders were scarce received, when they were openly violated at Dunkirk, and that too, *avec les circonstances les plus aggravantés* for what sir is the Fact, that cutter, about which I spoke to you again and again, is publickly suffered to go out of Dunkirk, Notwithstanding all my Representations, Notwithstanding a positive formal Promise from M de Maurepas to me, that she should not stir out of the Harbour, nay more, that Pirate Cunningham, so justly obnoxious to me, and whom M de Maurepas expressly promised to punish, is suffered to go on board Her, This Sir I mentioned to you on Thursday last, but I am now to add, what I did not know till last Night, and what will deserve all your attention. Scarce was Cunningham out of Dunkirk Harbour, when He began to cruize against us; He has taken several ships, one of them[2] has fallen again into our hands. The crew put on board of the Vessel consisted of one and twenty Persons, and sixteen of that number are Frenchmen, so that if that Proposition holds throughout, three-fourths of Cunningham's crew

1 Stevens's Facsimiles, Vol. XVI, No. 1597–1, 2, 10.
2 See p. 73.

AUGUSTATUS KUNINGAM

Fameux Marin Comodore au Service des Etats unis de l'Amerique et la terreur des Anglois

Gustavus Conyngham

are subjects of France,—on these Transactions so repug-
nant to every Principle of of Friendship, so contrary
to your most solemn Professions, the King my Master
orders me to make the strongest, and most serious
Representation. M de Vergennes seemed surprized,
and confounded, protested that they had been deceived
by the Admiralty of Dunkirk, and that to his certain
knowledge, the *Rapport* made was, that not a single
Frenchman was on board. He attempted no Justification, but on the contrary said, it was a thing against all
Rule, and directly contrary to His M. Xr[1] Majesty's
Intentions. I answered that when I had finished all I
had to say, I would produce my Proofs which I had in
my Pocket.

. . . .

I then shewed M de Vergennes the Papers I had
brought with me, which were the List of the sailors;
Cunningham Commission; his Letters to Messrs. Gardoqui, and Instructions to Captain Smith.[2] M de Vergennes answer was short but explicit, He said that they
had been grossly deceived with regard to the Dunkirk
Cutter, assured me, that the orders had been renewed
in the most Positive Terms, that can be used. I will tell
you in confidence added He, a Circumstance that shows
clearly the King's Intentions—After the Council that
was held Thursday Evening at Choisi, His Majesty
came up to M de Sartines and me, and said to M de Sartines, that He had heard that there was a Doubt in some
of the Ports how far the orders he had given were to be
strictly obeyed, Let them all know, that I expect the
strictest obedience. Upon this the orders were imme-

[1] Most Christian.
[2] James Smith, prize master of the brig Northampton. See p. 78.

diately renewed, I saw M de Sartines Letter, I desired to see it, not as suspecting in the least that He would wilfully express Himself in Ambiguous Terms, but I had sometimes observed a want of Vigour *dans ses Bureaux,* and wished to be sure that there was nothing of that kind on the present occasion. I have read the order, nothing can be clearer, or more positive, the different Officers are made Personally responsible for the Executive, beyond this it is impossible to go. I answered, that these orders if they were once known to be sincere, would be punctually obeyed, that I heartily wished, that might be the case, as it is upon that Executive that all depends. He pressed me to let him have copies of two of the Papers I had shown Him, with the List of the Sailors, and the Commission of the Congress to Cunningham. I saw no particular objection to this and therefore answered that tho' I had no orders I would take upon myself to comply with His Excellency's request.

I accordingly sent Him Copies of those two Papers yesterday Evening and accompanied them with a short note to which I have received the inclosed answer.

Your Lordship sees that in the Execution of the Important orders transmitted to me in your Letter No 48 I took nearly the same line I had taken a few Weeks ago on a similar occasion. I thought I could not do better than follow the same Plan, as my Conduct had met with His Majesty's most Gracious Approbation.

I am with the greatest Truth and Respect
My Lord
Your Lordships
Most Obedient
humble Servant STORMONT.

[LORD STORMONT TO LORD WEYMOUTH[1]]

(Extract)   Paris Saturday night
                              August 9, 1777

M de Maurepas seems really concerned for what passed at Dunkirk with regard to the Greyhound Cutter. Hodge and Allen[2] are confined in separate jails and the chef de Lamirauté is ordered hither to give an account of his conduct.

[COMTE DE VERGENNES TO THE MARQUIS DE NOAILLES[3]]

(Extract—Translation)
                              Versailles, 9 August 1777.

If the English Ministers will be sincere, they will admit that this difficulty or impossibility is common to them; at least we piously believe so, to save their good faith, otherwise, how should we explain so many disagreeable incidents from which we daily suffer. All that we respectively can do, then, is, whenever contraventions are recognized and proved, to grant most prompt and exact justice. That is the course we are

[1] Stevens's Facsimiles, Vol. XVII, No. 1644–7.
[2] Richard Allen.
[3] Stevens's Facsimiles, Vol. XVIII, No. 1646–2-6.

taking relative to the departure of Cunningham's vessel.

Explanation as to the device adopted by Captain Cunningham in order to obtain permission to leave Dunkirk.

I have already had the honour of informing you, Sir, of the devices adopted to induce the Admiralty of Dunkirk to permit the departure of that cutter. A subject of the King of England, named Richard Allen, presented himself as the purchaser of that vessel, the contract for the sale of which was passed by the Admiralty, and requested to be cleared for Bergen in Norway. The Admiralty, who had orders only to detain the privateer, seeing it assume the form of a merchantman, did not think themselves obliged to observe the same rigour, and were all the more easily persuaded to allow it to depart, as they thought by this means to prevent the scandal resulting from the threat of Mr. Frazer, who had declared to the Commandant that the English cutter had orders to destroy and burn that vessel anywhere, without any regard for the King's territory. I annex to this in proof, the letter which M. de Guichard, then Commandant at Dunkirk, wrote to me.

Letter from M. de Guichard annexed, proving the declaration made by Mr. Frazer that the Commandant of an English vessel had orders to burn Capt. Cunningham's vessel anywhere regardless of the King's territory.

The Admiralty thought it would obviate everything by taking security of the buyer and the seller that the vessel, having become English again, would not carry on privateering. I mention this detail not in order to justify the Admiralty, which presumed too much in taking on itself to interpret the King's orders, but to enable you to show the English Ministry that it was the threatening and insulting language of its officers which occasioned, and in a way necessitated the departure of the vessel.

The Admiralty, which has very precise orders to avoid anything which might compromise the good understanding between the two nations, understood that this would cease to exist, if the threat made by Mr. Frazer were carried out. This it wished to obviate, and thought of no better means of doing so than by removing the cause of the trouble. This foresight was doubtless out of its sphere, but as it cannot be supposed that Cunningham's departure should be the match we have prepared to kindle the flame of war, it is unquestionable that Captain Harvey's threat,[1] if carried out, would have been the most prompt signal, and that it would have taken place, failing the most complete satisfaction, —which it would probably not have been in the power of the British Ministry to give.

Explanation with Lord Stormont heated on his part, on the subject of the departure from Dunkirk of Cunningham's vessel.

In the explanation I had on the 5th. instant on this subject with Lord Stormont, and which was very heated on his part, I avoided speaking to him of Mr. Frazer's threatening declaration; I shall avoid even still more carefully in the future all discussion with him, because I have some reason to suspect that his views are not directed towards conciliation, and that, whether from a bad intention, or from fear of being mistaken, he always puts things in the worst light. One thing which strangely surprised me in him is that he ventured to attack by name M. de Sar-

[1] See pp. 62 and 63.

tine, whom he accuses of acting in opposition to the King's intentions. In their giving way to such personalities, he throws the reins to his zeal, especially when the imputations are only supported by reports which are almost always inexact. . . . Because the insurgents say that M. de Sartine is their friend,

We have reason to suspect that Lord Stormont's views are not directed towards conciliation. He has ventured to attack M. de Sartine by name with imputations.

because it has been supposed that this Minister, who is appointed to carry out the King's orders regarding the Navy, not being able to tolerate the continuance of the prizes in our ports, said.—"Why do they not take them to Spain or elsewhere?"—and because one of these prizes, which fell into the hands of the English, was sent to Bilboa, Viscount Stormont concluded positively that M. de Sartine had a regular understanding with the insurgents, that he was the soul of their councils, and the supporter of their views. . . .

Much patience is necessary, Sir, to listen calmly to such talk, my position obliges me not to lose it, and I am faithful to the obligation; thus, putting aside everything which could have given rise to sharp disputes, I limited myself to assuring Lord Stormont that, the King's sentiments being constantly the same, His Majesty was not disposed to allow things contrary to the friendship which he wishes to keep up with the King of Great Britain. I begged that Ambassador to give me a copy of the Commission which Cunningham handed to the person to whom he entrusted the Brigantine Northampton, and the list of Frenchmen found on board.

Order sent to Dunkirk to put Mr. Allen in prison, also the person who sold Mr. Cunningham's vessel.

The first of these documents was necessary to prove that, notwithstanding the assurance given, Cunningham has made some captures, and as Mr. Allen and the person who sold the vessel became security that he would make none, the King has caused orders to be sent to Dunkirk to arrest and put them in prison. But it remains to be seen whether they will be found there, and whether these people, who perhaps only had a temporary dwelling there, have not departed. It will not be long before we know.

Explanation on the subject of the sixteen Frenchmen who were found on board Capt. Cunningham's vessel.

With regard to the sixteen Frenchmen[1] found on board the Northumberland, I have much difficulty in believing that the officers of the Admiralty who attested here that they had allowed none to go on board Cunningham's vessel would have dared so impudently to deceive the Ministry; it is more likely that the sailors embarked out at sea, and hid themselves from the inspection of the Commissioners.

[1] See p. 74.

[M. LENOIR TO THE COMTE DE VERGENNES[1]]

(Translation)

Sir,   11 August 1777.

I have the honour to inform you that Mr. Hodge, an Anglo-American lodging in the Rue de Richelieu, at the Hotel de Vauban, was arrested this morning, and taken to the Bastille in execution of the King's orders.

I am with respect,
       Sir,
              Your very humble and
                     very obedient Servant

                                    LENOIR.

M. le Comte de Vergennes

[M. LENOIR TO THE COMTE DE VERGENNES[2]]

(Extract—Translation)   1777 11th. August

M. le Ray de Chaumont was anxious to know the causes of the detention.[3] I limited myself to saying that it was the King's order. He left me saying,—it is no doubt for the Cunningham (?) affair, they have wished

[1] Stevens's Facsimiles, Vol. XVIII, No. 1647.
[2] *Ibid.,* No. 1648–4.
[3] Of Hodge.

to give the small satisfaction to the English Ambassador. He added, moreover, that the Ambassador has spread a report that the Americans had been beaten, that they had lost four thousand men, and that their general had been killed, but that on this subject the Doctor[1] said *"Truth is one thing and Stormont another."*

Memoranda of Some of Lord Stormont's Correspondence[2]

(Extract)

15 August 1777 Lord Weymouth to Lord Stormont No. 50 Draft:—Acknowledges various letters—approves the sending to Count de Vergennes a list of the French sailors found on board Cunningham's prize and copy of that Captain's commission from the Congress[3] —refers to the French military force preparing for the West Indies, etc.

[1] Franklin.
[2] Stevens's Facsimiles, Vol. XVIII, No. 1702–2, 6, 7.
[3] See p. 81.

[MARQUIS DE NOAILLES TO THE COMTE DE VERGENNES [1]]

(Extract—Translation)

London 15 August 1777.

Complete satisfaction which we have given England by ordering the imprisonment of the seller and buyer of Cunningham's vessel.

Nothing better justifies our conduct than the detail which you have been good enough to give me of all that took place at Dunkirk from the entrance until the leaving of the vessel equipped by the American corsair Cunningham. If that corsair continues to make captures of the English, and to disturb their trade in the direction of the Baltic, we are by no means responsible. I remember now that Lord Weymouth told me about a month ago that it was proposed here to the Government to buy the vessel, adding that this expenditure would willingly be incurred, if by that means every sort of difficulty might be avoided. Why has this course not been adopted? They could then have prevented Mr. Richard Allen, who, although an English subject is alone guilty in this affair, from becoming the purchaser of this vessel, and no deception would have been practised on the Admiralty at Dunkirk, who thought they were only clearing a merchant vessel for Bergen in Norway. Moreover, as the purchaser and the seller, Mr. Hodge, according to orders which have been despatched, are to be put in prison, to make good their security. I think that we have done all that is possible on our part. Was the insolent threat of Captain Hervey

[1] Stevens's Facsimiles, Vol. XVIII, No. 1650–1, 3.

to be expected after that, of destroying all the American vessels, or all those which might be suspected of being such, wherever he might find them, without distinction of place?

[COMTE DE VERGENNES TO THE MARQUIS DE NOAILLES[1]]

(Extract—Translation)

Mr. Hodge, one of Cunningham's securities, arrested and put in the Bastille.

Refutation of Lord Weymouth's assertion that Cunningham ought never to have been released.

Versailles, 16 August 1777.

I have spoken to you so much at length in my preceeding despatches, Sir, of *Cunningham,* that I would not mention him here but to tell you that Mr. Hodge, one of his securities, having come to Paris, has been arrested and put in the Bastille, where he is at present, (and) if the remarks which Lord Weymouth made to you does not appear to require explanation He asserts that this Cunningham ought never to have been released. I should like to ask him from what code he takes this assertion. It is assuredly not from that of English laws, which could not be less favourable than they are to every kind of reciprocity. So we ought not to have punished Mr. Cunningham for the crimes of which he may have been guilty towards England or some Englishmen! If a prosecutor had presented himself to attack and prosecute, access to the tribunals would have

1 Stevens's Facsimiles, Vol. XVIII, No. 1651-1-3.

been open to him; but nobody appeared, so we could only punish for the offence which directly concerned us. The only grievance we had against him was that he

Very detailed explanation of our conduct regarding Cunningham.

cleared at the Customs as a smuggler, and returned as a privateer, which made him liable to be suspected of piracy; but, on due examination, he was in order in this respect—he had a commission. We had, therefore, nothing else to complain of than that he had concealed his real condition; for, with regard to his armament, he got it all complete from England. For this simple fact we kept him nearly a month in prison, and the tribunal, finding nothing to pronounce against him, set him at liberty pending further inquiry, a form of absolution which allows of no claim for damages or interest. The prizes which he had brought in were released and restituted by authority. It is astonishing that such marked demonstration of justice, and even of partiality, should excite complaints, instead of the gratitude which we had a right to expect. Lord Weymouth adds that he was set at liberty on an ill-chosen and insufficient security. There is a mistake here. Cunningham was set free without security, and there was no occasion to require any for him personally. That which the Admiralty took, some time before, had reference to the vessel, whose departure had been forbidden on the supposition that it was intended for privateering. The King is so little disposed to conceal this contravention of his orders that the Master Lieutenant of the Admiralty of Dunkirk has been ordered here to give an account of his conduct and his motives. They surely do not expect in England that we would punish people without hearing them; and orders have been given to arrest the two securities. Hodge, as I have just told you, is in the Bastille; he apparently thought to escape by coming to Paris, but he thereby hastened his imprisonment. I am not aware whether Mr. Richard Allen has been found at Dunkirk,—we expect news from there every moment.

Reasons which may make the Admiralty of Dunkirk excusable regarding the embarkation of sixteen Frenchmen on board Cunningham's vessel.

As regards the French sailors whom Cunningham must have taken on board, and of whom sixteen were found on the vessel when recaptured, it is very possible, Sir, that the Officers of the Admiralty are exempt from blame in this respect. You know the state of that port, and you are aware that beyond its boundary we have no power nor resources. It is very possible these people embarked in the roadstead or out at sea. It is because we cannot be sure of our sailors in that part that they are not brought under the laws of naval conscription (*Les classes*).

[LORD STORMONT TO LORD WEYMOUTH[1]]

(Extract)   Paris Augt. 20th. 1777

. . . In the course of my yesterdays Conversation with M de Vergennes . . . I told him, that I was by no means authorized to accept of this Proposal, and intimated that what passed at Dunkirk must beget in us very strong suspicions of all such sales. He answered with vivacity, that what had been done at Dunkirk gave us very just ground for complaint, but was in his opinion still more injurious to France: I gave this opinion added He this very Day to the King my Master, and told His Majesty that there was so much Stupidity in one part of the Admiralty of Dunkirk, and so much Knavery in the other, that I really did not know *s'il Lui falloit du foin ou des Verges,* this said He was I assure you the very Expression I used not an Hour ago, (I may observe to your Lordship here, that in this affair of Dunkirk, the french Ministers seem now to be in Earnest as Hodge is sent to the Bastille). M de Vergennes assured me, that the Purchase proposed was of a very Different Nature from that at Dunkirk, and that there could not be a possibility of fraud as it would be made by Frenchmen, Men of Substance, of whom the Ministers would be sure and for whom they could answer. I reported that I was not authorized to adopt this or any other Experiment, and that my orders were clear and precise, to demand that these ships might be immediately sent out of Port without convoy, and left to take their chance.

[1] Stevens's Facsimiles, Vol. XVIII, No. 1652–4, 5.

[COMTE DE VERGENNES TO THE MARQUIS
DE NOAILLES[1]]

(Extract—Translation)

Versailles, 23rd. August 1777

Escape of Mr. Richard Allen on Cunningham's vessel, for which he had become security.

Reasons which the Lieutenant-Governor of the Admiralty of Dunkirk gives in his defence upon the Cunningham affair.

I have already had the honour of informing you, Sir, with regard to the Dunkirk incident, that Mr. Hodge has been arrested. It was not possible to arrest Richard Allen, he had taken the precaution of embarking on the vessel for the destination of which he had become security. His escape certainly does no honour to the foresight of the Admiralty of Dunkirk. The president of that Board is here, and justifies himself by reasons which are half good and half bad. The Admiralty, not suspecting an understanding between Allen and Hodge, believed the sale of the vessel and its despatch to be purely a commercial affair. Neither Cunningham nor the French sailors were on board at the time of the examination; they must have been taken on board at sea. This justification is by no means improbable, in the opinion of those who know the condition of Dunkirk, its roadstead and its coast.

[1] Stevens's Facsimiles, Vol. XVIII, No. 1655–2.

[LORD STORMONT TO LORD WEYMOUTH[1]]

(Extract)   Paris Saturday Night Aug 23 1777

In my further conversation with him (Maurepas) his Excy mentioned Hodge being still confined in the Bastille. . . .

Hodge punished by being kept in the Bastille and the chef de Lamirauté punished by being ordered to attend the Court.

[SILAS DEANE TO ROBERT MORRIS[2][3]]

(Extract)   Paris, August 23rd, 1777

Soon after Mr. Hodge's arrival, we bought a lugger at Dover, and sent her to Dunkirk. Mr. Hodge went after her, and equipped her with great secrecy, designing a blow in the North Sea. He sent Captain Cunningham in her, and ordered him to intercept the packet between England and Holland, and then to cruise northward toward the Baltic. Cunningham fell in with the packet in a day or two after leaving Dunkirk, and

[1] Stevens's Facsimiles, Vol. XVIII, No. 1654–8, 16.
[2] Vice-President of the Marine Committee and a member of the Continental Congress.
[3] MSS. Department of State; printed in Wharton's Diplomatic Correspondence, Vol. II, pp. 378–382.   [4] The Surprize.

took her. As she had a prodigious number of letters on board, he imagined it was proper he should return to Dunkirk instead of continuing his course. In his return he also took a brig of some value, and brought both prizes into port. This spread the alarm far and wide, and gave much real ground of complaint, as he had been entirely armed and equipped in Dunkirk, and had returned thither with his prizes. The ministry, therefore, to appease England, ordered the prizes to be returned, and Cunningham and his crew to be imprisoned, which gave the English a temporary triumph.

But not discouraged thereby, another cutter[1] was bought, and equipped completely in the port of Dunkirk. Cunningham and his crew were set at liberty, and with some address and intrigue he got again to sea from the same port, in a swift-sailing cutter, mounting fourteen six pounders and twenty-two swivels, with one hundred and six men. His first adventure greatly raised insurance on the northern trade: even the packet-boats from Dover to Calais were for some time insured. On his leaving the port of Dunkirk the second time, he had orders to proceed directly for America; but he and his crew, full of resentment for the insults they had received from the enemy whilst in prison at Dunkirk and afterwards, attacked the first vessels they met with, and plundered and burnt as they went on. Our last accounts are, that they had taken or destroyed about twenty sail, and had appeared off the town of Lynn, and threatened to burn it unless ransomed; but the wind proving unfavorable, they could not put their threats into execution. In a word, Cunningham, by his first and second

---

[1] The Revenge.

bold expeditions, is become the terror of all the eastern coast of England and Scotland, and is more dreaded than Thurot was in the late war. But though this distresses our enemies, it embarrasses us. We solicited his enlargement; and Mr. Hodge engaged for his going directly for America. I know now how his engagement was expressed, but to appease the British ministry, and drive off an instant war, Mr. Hodge has been arrested and confined. His friends need not be in distress for him: he will soon be at liberty. He merits much from his country, having been ready at all times to promote and serve its interests.

[M. DE GUICHARD TO THE COMTE DE VERGENNES[1]]

(Translation)
M. de Rayneval

Dunkirk 25 August 1777

Monseigneur

Testimony given by M de Guichard
in the conduct of M d'Hersin.

I have the honour to inform you that I have just learnt that M d'Hersin, Lieutenant-General of the Admiralty of this town has been charged by the Court to give an account of his conduct concerning the ship Greyhound, of which Mr. Hodge is the owner, and which left here on the 17th. of last month. It is said M d'Hersin is accused of having countenanced the emi-

[1] Stevens's Facsimiles, Vol. XVIII, No. 1657–1.

gration of the King's subjects in favour of the American vessel. I had the honour, Monseigneur, to inform you on the 20th July of this year of all that passed on that occasion; every possible precaution was taken in order that no Frenchmen should embark on the Greyhound, but as I had the honour of informing you, if in the country, on the coast, or in the dunes, during the night, some Frenchmen might have hidden, who would find means of reaching the vessel, such a thing is not possible to foresee or prevent. No doubt someone has contrived to cast suspicion on M. d'Hersin's conduct. He enjoys here the reputation of a man who fulfils his duties with exactitude. For my part, I regard him as incapable of neglecting the orders of the Court.

I am with very profound respect

Monseigneur

Your very humble and

very obedient Servant

DE GUICHARD

Memoranda of Some of Lord Stormont's Correspondence[1]

10 September 1777 Lord Stormont to Lord Weymouth No. 141:—That he had told Count de Vergennes there was reason to believe that the pirate Cunningham intended returning to some port in France with the

[1] Stevens's Facsimiles, Vol. XVIII, No. 1702–6.

prizes—Vergennes replied in such a way as to leave no doubt that Cunningham would be punished according to his deserts.

[COMTE DE VERGENNES TO THE MARQUIS
DE NOAILLES[1]]

(Extract—Translation)

Paris, 13th. September 1777.

I saw Lord Stormont on the 9th.; our meeting had no object, and he had no complaints to make. I could have made some myself to him, but I reserve them for you for next week, not yet having all the explanations which are necessary. This ambassador says he has information that the famous Cunningham is preparing to return to our ports; I doubt it, for he could not do a worse thing.

Statement of Moneys Expended on the Revenge[2]

(Translation)

Account of the various expenditures made by Mr. Miguel Lagaonere and company of Corunna for the expenses, repairs and lodging of the armed sloop of war named the Revenge, property of the Congress of the thirteen United States of America, Capt. Gustavus Conyngham who brought his vessel into port in the Ria del ferrol, as follows

[1] Stevens's Facsimiles, Vol. XVIII, No. 1684–4.
[2] MSS. in the collection of Mr. James Barnes.

French Print showing Britannia upbraiding Neptune and pointing to Conyngham, while the English fleet are in full flight, Victory deserting them

Itemized

For a large mast 46 cubits long, five planks, iron nails, pitch, tar, grease and various other things, details taken from the maritime warehouses of Corunna according to the account submitted by the Captain of the Navy Yard keeper of the warehouse. Amount   9025 " 16

For the wages of carpenters employed to make the large mast according to the account and receipt signed by Domingo de Murcia, foreman of carpenters employed in the Navy Yard Workshop   691 " 00

For the export duties of the large mast and one of the planks, paid to the Royal Customs House of Coruna, and a real for the porter   607 " 21

For four cwt. of cheese bought from Messrs. Gerner & Co., according to receipt   800 " 00

For twelve measures of white beans according to receipt of Ant. Montero   192 " 00

For four cwt. of Levant rice according to receipt of Franco. Pissang & Company   432 " 00

For two barrels of French flour bought from Messrs. Lagoanerey & Co.   320 " 00

For one barrel of vinegar according to receipt of Mr. Isidro Dalmon   225 " 00

For two cwt of broken sugar according to receipt of Mr. Ftys. de Llano   344 " 00

For twenty five lbs of wax candles bought from Mr Peter Marick   238 " 00

Carried forward   12765 " 03

Brought forward   12765 " 03

For eight barrels of Rum and Case Brandy of six pipes bought from Mr Joseph Manoy Murrietta at twelve pesos a barrel   1920 " 00

Paid to the Royal Customs House of Corunna for export duties of all the foregoing comestibles, including a real for the porter   502 " 33

For three different barrels for the beans and rice   5 " 00

For three wagons for transport to the Customs House of all comestibles, including the boy and the embarking on board the sloop   28 " 00

For freightage of the barge which transported the mast and comestibles to Ferrol as put down   20 " 00

For the following bought in Ferrol and charged to the account of Mr Miguel Lagoanere & Co.

    40 cwt. and 35 lbs of captain's biscuit at 100 ron a cwt.   4035 " 00

    25 cwt & 35 lbs salt pork at 2 40 r. a cwt.   3684 " 00

    25 cwt & 77 lbs of salt beef at 1 40 r cwt   2207 " 27   9926 " 27

For   Customs
House duties for
these three arti-
cles   2352 " 00
For going to Alca-
rala   200 " 00
Cartage of grain
and portage   20 " 00 1562 " 00
                                    11488 " 27

For amount of various sums of money delivered to Capt. Conyngham according to
his nine receipts collected by Mr John
Lembeye of Ferrol who charged them to
the account of Messrs. Lagoanere & Co.   9288 " 00

                                    36127 " 29
For commission for disbursements and an
interest at 4%   1445 " 05

                                  37573 "
Money deducted that we have had delivered to us by Captain Conyngham   12000

                      Total 25573
                    copper Reales

                    Proved

Error and Omission: We certify the foregoing account
which amounts to Twenty five thousand five hundred
and seventy three copper reales, and we have received
a draft for the same amount payable at forty days

drawn by Mr Gustavus Conyngham to our order and charged on Messrs. Gardoqui and Sons of Bilbao payable in Madrid, for first, second and third: and in settlement of which we sign this. Ferrol sixteenth of September one thousand seven hundred and seventy seven.

For Messrs. Migl. Lagoanere & Co.
= Miguel Lagoanere
Toben.

I, Gustav Conyngham acknowledge that Messrs Lagoanere & Company of Coruna have made the disbursements mentioned in this account, amounting to the Sum of Twenty Five thousand Five hundred and seventy three copper reales, for the payment of which I have given them a draft for the same amount payable at forty days to the order of Messrs. Gardoqui & Son of Bilbao, payable in Madrid, and in payment of which I pledge in case of need, my person, my belongings present and future, and generally and especially the armed sloop of war the Revenge which I command and the prizes and ransoms that I have already taken and will take in virtue of a commission from the Congress of the thirteen United States of America which I hold. Desiring and expecting that the present obligation will have the same force as if it had been signed before a notary. In faith of which I have signed it and for greater authenticity I have also had it signed as a witness by the chief officer of my staff, made in triplicate at Ferrol the same day and year as above.

G. CONYNGHam
THOMAS HEASE

[LORD STORMONT TO LORD WEYMOUTH[1]]

(Extract)   Paris Sept. 17th 1777

I have pretty good reason to believe that Beaumarchais is at present upon very bad terms with Franklin & Deane. They impute to his indiscretion the Discovery of all that Hodges did at Dunkirk, & upbraid him with being the original cause of Hodge's imprisonment.

Memoranda of Some of Lord Stormont's Correspondence[2]

19 September 1777   Lord Weymouth to Lord Stormont. No. 58 Draft. . . . His Majesty is willing to believe the professions made by the French King are sincere and that the several late regulations respecting the rebel privateers will be observed. A postscript states that it is reported from Corunna that Cunningham has arrived at Ferrol where he is allowed to refit.

[1] Stevens's Facsimiles, Vol. XVIII, No. 1687–1.
[2] *Ibid.,* No. 1702–7.

[LAGOANERE & CO.[1] TO PIERRE LAPEIRE, MERCHANT[2]]

(Translation.)

Corunna the 19. September. 1777

Mr. Pierre Lapeire in Vigo

Sir

We are giving this letter to Capt. Gustavus Conyngham commanding the armed vessel of war, named the Revenge belonging to the Congress of the Thirteen United Provinces of America, to beg you to be so kind as to render all the services within your power to the Captain and to those who may come from his part, requesting you likewise to make such disbursements for our account as he or his representatives may be in need of, giving us immediate advices of the same that we may reimburse them to you. You may count on our gratitude as well as on the perfect regard with which we have the honor to be

Sir

Your very humble & very
obedient servants

LAGOANERE & COMP.

[1] The American agents at Corunna, Spain.
[2] MSS. in the collection of Mr. James Barnes.

[LAGOANERE & CO. TO ALEXORDE CATARELO[1]]

(Translation)

My dear Sir:

We herewith present Captain Gustavus Conyngham of the armed sloop of war named the Revenge property of the Congress of the thirteen United States of America, to request you to be so good as to favor the said Captain, and also the persons whom he will recommend to you, as much as depends on you. Asking you also to put down to our account all the expenditures that he, and those whom he recommends, may require, advising us of the amount in order that we may remit it to you immediately.

You may count on our gratitude as on the true affection with which we pray God to protect you.

Coruna 19th September 1777.

B. L. M. de V M.
Your obedient servants
MIGL. LAGOANEREY AND CO

Mr. Domingo fernando
Alexorde Catarelo.
Rivadeo

---

[1] MSS. in the collection of Mr. James Barnes.

[LAGOANERE & CO. TO BLAS. PARGA VACUMONDE[1]]

(Translation)

My dear Sir:

We herewith present Captain Gustavus Conyngham who is in command of the armed sloop of war named the Revenge, belonging to the Congress of the thirteen United States of America, to request you to be so good as to favor the said Captain, and also the persons whom he will recommend to you, as much as depends on you. Asking you also to put down to our account all the expenditures that he, and those whom he recommends, may require, advising us of the amount in order that we may remit it to you immediately.

You may count on our gratitude as on the true affection with which we pray God to protect you.

Coruna 19th. September 1777.

B. L. M. de V M

Your obedient servants

MIGL. LAGOANERY AND CO.

Mr. Blas. Parga Vacumonde
Vivero

[SILAS DEANE TO MESSRS. LAGOANERE & CO.[2]]

Paris, Septr. 20th, 1777.

Gentlemen,—

Your Favor of the 30th. ulto. I received & am much obliged to you for the Favors shown Capt. Cunningham, who I hoped indeed had gone direct to America,

---

1 MSS. in the collection of Mr. James Barnes.

2 In The Deane Papers, Collections of the New-York Historical Society, Vol. II, p. 140.

but conclude he must have met with some misfortune in his voyage, which obliged him to go to Spain. The Necessary articles to repair his vessel for the voyage are, I hope, by this Time supplied, for which Capt. Cunningham's Bills on Messr. Gardroquis[1] of Bilboa will be honored, as they have been wrote to on the subject. I thank you for your kind offers of Service, & have the honor to remain, with the highest Esteem,

Gentlemen, yours etc.,

S. Deane.

Messrs. Lagoanen & Co.,[2] Mecrts., Coruna, Spain.

[M. AMELOT[3] TO THE COMTE DE VERGENNES[4]]

(Translation)

M. de Rayneval   Paris, 24 September 1777.

Liberty granted to Mr. Hodge
Cunningham's security.

The Comte de Maurepas has told me, Sir, that the King's intention, as settled by you with His Majesty, was to set at liberty Mr. Hodge, an Englishman, detained in the Bastille by his orders. I have the honour to inform you that I have in consequence just given those necessary for his release.

I have the honour to be with perfect attachment, Sir,
your very humble
and very obedient servant

M. de Vergennes.   Amelot.

[1] Gardoqui.   [2] Lagoanere & Co.
[3] Minister of the Household to Louis XVI.
[4] Stevens's Facsimiles, Vol. XVIII, No. 1694.

[LORD STORMONT TO LORD WEYMOUTH[1]]

(Extract)

Paris 25 Septr. 1777.

—Hodge is set at Liberty.—

[COMTE DE VERGENNES TO M. AMELOT[2]]

(Translation)

M. Amelot.

Versailles, 26 September 1777.

Liberty given to
Mr. Hodge, Mr.
Cunningham's
security.

  I have received, Sir, the letter which you did me the honour to write to me on the 24th. instant. I thank you for the notice you have been good enough to give me of the King's orders regarding Mr. Hodge, an American who had been detained in the Bastille.

[ARTHUR LEE TO ROBERT MORRIS[3]]

(Extract)

Paris Oct. 4th. 1777

  Mr. Dean has determined to give you an account of the fitting out & directing Cunningham's vessel, at Dunkirk, which has done so much injury here, & caused the

[1] Stevens's Facsimiles, Vol. XVIII, No. 1700.
[2] *Ibid.,* Vol. XIX, No. 1703.
[3] *Ibid.,* No. 1714–3.

late unfriendly measures. We are unable to explain it in conjunction, because it was done by Mr. Dean without our knowledge. It will not however be fair to judge of this Court by measures, which they have taken unwillingly as they assure us, & from the necessity produced principally by this illegal transaction.

[ARTHUR LEE[1] TO RICHARD HENRY LEE[2][3]]

(Extract)   4 October 1777

I enclose you a copy of a late measure of the Court here wch. seems unfavorable to us. The reason they give for it is our having armd Cunningham in their port & sent him to cruize in the Channel, contrary to their treaty, to their repeated requests & our promises. The fact is so, & it was done by Mr. Deane without consultg. or informing us. He has therefore thought it necessary to write an apology for it, which I understand is to be shown about privately, & he seems desirous of persuading us & others to be in ill-humour with the Court for taking violent measures to which they have been compeld by his unwarrantable conduct. All I can say is, that it will be doing them great injustice to form an opinion of their disposition, from steps which they assure us were taken from necessity, & to which We are conscious those proceedings forced them.

[1] United States Commissioner to France.
[2] Chairman of the Marine Committee and delegate to the Continental Congress.
[3] Stevens's Facsimiles, Vol. III, No. 269–6-7.

American Commissioners—Sketch of Disbursements[1]

(Extract)   [About 7 October 1777]

To Mr. Hodge for equipment of the } 60000 Livres
Two Cutters at Dunkirk   }

[FRANKLIN, DEANE, AND LEE TO THE COMMITTEE
OF FOREIGN AFFAIRS[2]]

(Extract)   Passy, October 7, 1777.

Mr. Hodge is discharged from his imprisonment on our solicitation, and his papers restored to him; he was well treated while in the Bastile. The charge against him was, deceiving the Government in fitting out Cunningham from Dunkirk, who was represented as going on some trading voyage; but as soon as he was out began a cruise on the British coast, and took six sail. He is got safe into Ferrol.

[1] Stevens's Facsimiles, Vol. III, No. 272–1.
[2] MSS. Department of State; printed in Wharton's Diplomatic Correspondence of the American Revolution, Vol. II, p. 406.

Intelligence probably collected in Paris[1] and delivered to Lord Suffolk[2]

(Extract)   [About 17 October 1777]

When he left Dunkirk his vessel mounted 14 carriage & 22 swivel guns, having 106 Seamen 66 of which were Frenchmen, Entered with an obligation to return in three months to Dunkirk.

Cunningham has again sailed from Ferrol on a Cruizer—after selling His Prizes—he says for half price—& refitting His Ship the Revenge—He procured Papers from a Mercht there (which were intended for another Ship belonging to Spain) to Cover the Black Prince—a Prize—laden with wine, Fruit & oyl which he sent to Bayonne.

[SILAS DEANE TO JOHN ROSS[3]]

Dear Sir,—   Paris, 19th. Novr., 1777.

Mr. Hodge went for Dunkirk on Saturday; he will return, I expect tomorrow. The Little Vessel in which Capt. Cunningham formerly sailed is by Mr. Chaumont ordered round to L'Orient. I mention this, as she

---

[1] By Paul Wentworth.
[2] Stevens's Facsimiles, Vol. III, No. 274–7.
[3] In The Deane Papers, Collections of the New-York Historical Society, Vol. II, p. 227.

may probably answer for Mr. Hodge to take a passage in, if no objections are made to his going in her, which I am apprehensive of, & that the objections will Lye equally against the Dolphin, on account of their having been formerly employed in a Cruize,[1] & on Mr. Hodge's account, on whose motions our Enemies have a jealous Eye; consequently his taking a passage in either of them, however innocent his attentions may be, will unavoidably, if observed & complained of, occasion difficulties of which you ought to be apprized. Both the Dolphin & Luggar were long since prohibited going out as American property, unless to America or some foreign Port. The Commissioners have ordered the Dolphin to be sold, & it is indifferent to them who purchases her. If you think she will suit you either to send to America or any foreign port on any business, except that of Cruizing against the English, advise you to purchase her, otherwise not. But I will discourse with Mr. Hodge on his return, and write you the result, as well as what he may do at Dunkirk. I saw Mr. Moylan last evening, and since received a Letter from Mr. Williams, informing that Mr. Gourlade had applied to him on the same subject. I have replied to Mr. Williams that Mr. Moylan had been spoken to by you when here, & by Mr. W. Lee since, on the subject. It is indifferent to me personally, but shall be sorry for any interference, real or apparent.

I am, etc.,

Mr. Jno. Ross.   SILAS DEANE.

[1] Around Ireland in company with the Reprisal and Lexington.

[LAGOANERE & CO. TO LASSORE & CO., MERCHANTS[1]]

(Translation)

Corunna the 28 November 1777

M. Lassore brother & Compe. in Cadiz

Gentlemen

Captain Gustavus Cunyngham commanding the Cutter of War named the Revenge belonging to the Congress of the Thirteen United Provinces of America having asked us for a recommendation for your city, we are giving him this letter by which we beg you to be so kind as to render him every service within your power in case he should find himself obliged to put into your port and to furnish him with whatever money he may be in need of to refit his vessel. He will hand you drafts on the deputies of the Congress in Paris or on his other correspondents, or on us. We shall be under the greatest obligation to you for the services you may be able to render him & have the honor to be, with perfect consideration, Gentlemen

Your very humble
& very obedient servants
LAGOANERE & COMP.

[1] MSS. in the collection of Mr. James Barnes.

[SILAS DEANE TO JOHN ROSS[1]]

(Extract)   Paris, Decr. 1st., 1777.

Cunningham has lately carried another Prize into Spain, loaded with Fish, and Suffer'd himself, in a Gale of Wind, on accot. of his Mast being too large; he was altering it, & getting ready for another Cruize. The Letter from thence was dated the 12th. Novr.

[SILAS DEANE TO MESSRS. LEOGANERE[2]]

                                             Paris, Decr. 2d., 1777.
Gentlemen,—
Yours of the 12th. of Novr. I received, & return you my thanks for your kind attention to our affairs in your Port. This will be handed you by Mr. Hodge, a Gentleman of Philadelphia, whom I recommend to your civilities. He is empowered to take the care and direction of Capt. Cunningham's Vessel, and it is with pleasure, I assure you, that you may rely on him as a person well acquainted with American affairs, and on whose information you may depend. I shall be happy in the continuance of your correspondence. I am, etc.

Messrs. Leoganere & Co.   SILAS DEANE.

[1] In The Deane Papers, Collections of the New-York Historical Society, Vol. II, p. 259.
[2] *Ibid.*, p. 263.

[SILAS DEANE TO JOHN ROSS[1]]

(Extract)   Paris, Decemr. 18th., 1777.

I this moment received a Letter from Cunningham.
He was at Corrunna the 27th. Novr., doing very well,
having got Liberty to sell his prize openly, & was pushing out on a fresh Cruise.

Memorandum of Intelligence[2] [3]

(Extract)   [About 24 December 1777]

Cunningham lately carryed a prize to Corruna & sold
her publickly—

Extract from the London Annual Register for 1778[4]

When a bold American adventurer, one Cunningham, had taken and carried into Dunkirk, with a privateer fitted out at that port, the English packet from
Holland, and sent the mail to the American ministers

---

[1] In The Deane Papers, Collections of the New-York Historical
Society, Vol. II, p. 280.

[2] Obtained by Paul Wentworth.

[3] Stevens's Facsimiles, Vol. VII, No. 721–1.   [4] Page 37.

at Paris, it then seemed necessary in some degree to discountenance so flagrant a violation of good neighborhood, as well as of the standing treaties between the two nations, and even of the particular marine laws and regulations established in France, in regard to her conduct with the people of other countries. Cunningham and his crew were accordingly committed for some short time to prison. Yet this appearance of satisfaction was done away by the circumstances which attended it. For Cunningham's imprisonment was represented to the Americans, as proceeding merely from some informality in his commission, and irregularity in his proceedings, which had brought him to, if not within, the verge of piracy, and which were too glaring to be entirely passed over without notice. And he was, with his crew, not only speedily released from their mock confinement, but he was permitted to purchase, fit out, and arm a much stronger vessel, and better sailer than the former, avowedly to infest as before the British commerce.

[SILAS DEANE TO JOHN ROSS[1]]

(Extract)

Paris, 15th. Jan'y, 1778

Cunningham had, on the 20th. December, carried in two prizes to Carogne, one of which sold for 6,000 & the other for 4,500, & was gone out on a second Cruize.

[1] In The Deane Papers, Collections of the New-York Historical Society, Vol. II, p. 331.

[GARDOQUI & SONS TO GUSTAVUS CONYNGHAM[1]]

Bilbao the 17th Janry 1778

Capt Gustavus Cuningham—

Sir

By your very agreable & esteem'd favour of the 14th. Instant are glad to see the fair disposition your affair stands in, thro' the assistance of the Gentlemen you are recommended to, & flatter ourselves that they will be able to compleatt the same to your Intire satisfaction. We suppose you are allready informd that the Cutter departted hence on Tuesday last in order to retack if posible a Tobaco Brigg that was given up by the forgery of the Spanish Pylott to a Jersey Privateer not further than a Muskett shott from the Spanish land which resolution we had the pleasure to be approved of by our worthy Freind Mr. Hoadge who arrived safe in Towne the day before yesterday, as such doubt not your being pleased therewith, Expecially when have to informe you that the same day that she went out she fell in, & tooke a ship from the Land bound to this port with 2373 Quintales of fish & 59 Tons of oyl on Board of whome Capt Beach putt in as a prize Master Jeremiah Hibbert Master of one of the American Privateers in the river who went as a Volunteer in the Cutter; the ship tho' believed bound to this place has not yet made her ap-

---

[1] MSS. in the collection of Mr. James Barnes.

pearance with us, butt when does, depend on our giving you punctuall advice, mean while remmain with sincere reggards   Sir.   your mh. obt hble Serts.

JOSEPH GARDOQUI & SONS

We are this Instant informed that the Prize ship is safe in our river aGoverno

[SILAS DEANE TO GUSTAVUS CONYNGHAM[1]]

Sir,—   Paris, 21st. Jany., 1778.

I received your letter of the 4th. inst., and consulted on the contents with my Colleagues. It is very unlucky that you fell in with that Vessel. Every such adventure gives our Enemies advantage against us by representing us as persons who regard not the Laws of Nations. Your Idea that you are at Liberty to seize English Property on board of French[2] or other neutral Vessels is wrong; it is contrary to the established Laws among the maritime Powers in Europe, tho' it is true that the English, in the last war, paid little or no regard to this Law, but their superiority at sea carried them thro'. They have practiced the same this war, but their situation and ours is very different in point of Force, tho' not so in point of right. You will, therefore, represent the case to the Admiralty just as it was conducted, as you have represented in your Letter to us, & drop your claim; & in future let French, Spanish & other Neutral Vessels pass without detaining of them, unless you find them loaded with warlike stores & bound to the Ports of our Enemy, in which Case only they may be detained agreeable to the Laws & Treaties between the Maritime States

[1] In The Deane Papers, Collections of the New-York Historical Society, Vol. II, p. 340.   [2] See p. 123.

in Europe. I hope Mr. Hodge is with you by this time, who can give you more particulars than is proper for me to write. Wishing you Success, I am, with Esteem,

Yours, etc.,

Capt. Cunningham.

SILAS DEANE.

P.S. I have not as yet received the Ransom Money, nor have I any answ. to my last Letter on the Subject, in which I sent forward the letter of the Hostage, & a Copy of yours to me.

[SILAS DEANE TO MESSRS. LAGOANERE[1]]

Sir,—

Paris, Feby. 17th., 1778.

By a Billet I this moment received from my Colleague Mr. Lee, I learn you had not received my answer to yours respecting Capt. Cunningham's Prizes You, who are on the Place, must be the judge of what is proper & what can be done, and the Commissioners have the fullest (confidence) in you that every necessary step will be pursued to obtain the delivery of those Prizes, and that they will be disposed of to the best advantage. The last news from America gave us most favourable accounts of the situation of our Forces, though nothing of Consequence had happened at the close of the month of December, when the armies were still in the Field. Permit me to recommend the Bearer, Capt. Courten, to your Civilities, & as he setts out this instant, I have no time to add, save that I am, with the utmost respect, Dear Sir,

Your most obedient & very Humble Servt.,

Messrs. Ligoniere & Co.

SILAS DEANE.

[1] In The Deane Papers, Collections of the New-York Historical Society, Vol. II, p. 375.

[WILLIAM HODGE TO JOHN ROSS[1]]

Bilboa, Feb'y, 19th, 1778.

Dear Sir,—

You will probably think that I have been very neglectfull in not writing to you oftener, and the only apology that I can offer is, that I have been engaged in the most troublesome affair that ever I undertook, and had I expected that I should have had half the trouble to Encounter with, the Cutter might have remained in Bilboa, before I would have taken the Management of her; but as I engaged with you and Mr. Deane that I would take charge of her, I am determined that nothing shall be wanting on my part. All our seamen had left the Cutter before my Arrival at Bilboa, but the New England seamen, going on board to pursue the Tobacco Brig, occasioned our people to go on board likewise; but as soon as she returned to St. Anthonys, our people again left the Vessell. I immediately went up to St. Anthony, and when I went on board, there were a greater number of prisoners than our Men, and its being an open port, I wonder that they did not take the Vessell from our people. After my going on board with six Men as a reinforcement, there was still danger, but thank God, we brought her safe into Bilboa, and I have had nothing but trouble with our people ever since. I have been obliged to settle with them for their wages and prize Money, and after all one half have left the Vessell. The wages and disbursements upon the Cutter amounts to Pieces of Vellon 109,284, and the

[1] In The Deane Papers, Collections of the New-York Historical Society, Vol. II, p. 376.

share of prize Money to the officers and crew Amounts to 137,750 Pieces of Vellon besides their share of prize Money of the ship Hope and Cargo (which was brought into this port since my Arrival), in which they shared one third; and forty-two Volunteers who shared at the rate of one half the ship Hope, Nr. Pieces of Vellon 239,458.24, which Money, together with some more, I have been obliged to take up to discharge the demands against the Cutter. A letter from the Honl. Arthur Lee, Esqr., to Capt. Conyngham has been of considerable detriment to me, and has puzzled me to know how to act in regard to the Accounts; it appears very artfull and wicked, As well as a Letter he wrote to Corrunna, likewise one wrote to the Gardoques, who he desires to furnish the Cutter with a Credit only for one half of her disbursements and charges as only half he says belongs to the Congress. I shall Enclose you a Copy of the Letter to Mr. Ligoniere at Corunna and likewise a Copy of the letter to Captain Conyngham. I hope you will employ your pen with these Gentleman, and send the Copy to Mr. Deane.

The Vessell is very indifferently manned, nevertheless I shall set sail to morrow for Martinique, to which place I hope you will write me, and inform me what answer you have from Arthur Lee, Esqr. Mr. Roach, our first Lieutenant, has left us, and will be with you in a few weeks; he will be a proper person to take charge of the Cutter that is with you, if she is not disposed off. I would recommend that you would send her to Martinique if she is delivered up to us. Capt. Conyngham, unfortunately taking the French Brig,[1] has been the

---

[1] See p. 120.

occasion of upwards of Ten Thousand dollars being stopped in our friends hands at Corunna, and how the affair will End I know not. I shall leave Capt. Conyngham's accounts of wages and disbursements upon the Cutter to be forwarded you by Messr. Gardoques. I am obliged to hurry out of the port, as it is possible that an order may come against the Cutter, in consequence of her taking the French Brig. Capt. Conyngham requests me to inform you that there is a ballance due him, and in case any accident should happen, that you would take care that his wife might receive it. My Compliments to all friends, And accept the same from your friend and humble Servt.,

W. HODGE.

Mr. John Ross.

[MR. COURTEN TO SILAS DEANE[1]]

(Extract—Translation)

March 13 1778

Messrs. Leogene render me every possible service, and have begged me to look upon their house as my own. They have told me that Captain Cunningham and Mr. Hoge were at Bilboa, and that they expected them at Corunna.

[1] Stevens's Facsimiles, Vol. VIII, No. 801–2.

[THE AMERICAN COMMISSIONERS TO GUSTAVUS
CONYNGHAM[1]]

Sir   Paris April 19th 1778

We have received a Complaint from the remaining
part of your officers and Crew, of an unfair distribution
of prize Money by Mr. Hodge. To prevent any such
Complaints in future we desire that you will put your
prizes into the Hands of Messieurs Gardoqui at Bilboa,
and into those of the principal Merchants at Cadiz or
Corogne, directing them to make a speedy distribution
of the prize Money among the Crew and account to us
for the public part. You will inform us, at the same
time of their Contents and what they are supposed to be
worth.

We wish to have immediately an account of what you
have hitherto taken, their supposed value and to whom
committed. You will use your utmost endeavours to
make up your Crew and taking a Cruise where you can
with safety, come to Bourdeaux, Brest or Nantes. We
can there examine into your Disputes and settle your
future Establishment, with much more ease and effect.

Where you make a prize you should take Copies of
her Bills of Loading or an Inventory of her Contents;
by sending Us Copies of which we can check the Mer-

---

[1] MSS. in the Papers of the Continental Congress—Letters of
John Adams, 84, Vol. I, p. 149 (Bureau of Rolls and Library, Department of State).

chants account and prevent any Imposition. We wish to be favoured with a Copy of your Commission. We are x

To Capt. Cunningham of the Revenge at Cadiz.

N.B. You will inform your Ships Company of the directions we have given to provide for their Satisfaction in future.

[LETTER TO MESSRS. JOS. AND GEORGE AUDIBEN[1]]

(Translation)

Cadiz, April 14, 1778.

Gentlemen:

Mr. Conyngham commanding the American privateer The Revenge, counting on leaving this port to go into the Mediterranean,—to send the prizes he may take from the English into Marseilles, for sale,—has asked me to procure for him in the said town the name of a business house, to whom he can apply with confidence. We believe, gentlemen, we could not recommend a better house than yours, and we shall be obliged if you will render him any services he may require. We are depending on you to arrange the same and on all other occasions for those who have the honor to be, with the greatest consideration,

Your very humble and obedient servants,

Messrs. Jos. and George Audiben.

[1] In the collection of Mr. James Barnes.

*Extract of a Letter from an Officer on Board the
Monarch, lately arrived at Portsmouth
from her Cruize.*[1]

We are at length, thank heaven, arrived once more in
an English port. Our last foreign port was Cadiz,
where we experienced such treatment as will scarce be
credited; though the vouchers which government will
receive by another channel, as well as ours, will surely
set them on a scheme to resent the insult offered to a
King's ship. We came into Cadiz harbour on the Sunday afternoon, when the Captain, according to custom,
ordered the boat on shore to get what is termed product,
which could not be obtained: the next day another was
sent, and a third, and a fourth; but to all we could not
even get an answer. A spirited memorial was at last
sent to the commandant, who also gave no answer; in
short, they seemed resolved to take no notice of us.
Judge of the situation of our spirited commander (who
is a true British seaman) when during the time we lay
there (seven days being detained by the wind) we had
the mortification to see the usual honours paid to two
Dutch frigates, and above all to the Revenge American privateer, commanded by Cunningham, who came
swaggering in with his thirteen stripes, saluted the
Spanish admiral, had it returned, and immediately got
product; the Spaniards themselves carrying on board
wood, water, fruit, and fresh provisions; all which we

[1] In the London Chronicle for 1778, May 5–7, p. 439.

were eye-witnesses of, as he anchored directly under our stern, within two cables length. There are at Cadiz twenty-two ships of war of the line, besides frigates and chebecs: the first are as fine vessels to look at as ever put to sea: they all appear full manned, and are deep in the water, as if provided with all necessaries ready to put to sea on the shortest notice. There were also riding here eleven vessels bearing the American flag; and six more ships of war were expected daily from Ferrol to join the above fleet, which we were informed of by the Captain of one of the Dutch frigates, who behaved barely civil to us. We were happy on our coming up to Spithead, to see so fine a fleet ready to chastise our insolent and natural enemies. I am so far from exaggerating the account of our reception at Cadiz, that I have been obliged to omit some very humiliating circumstances that happened during our stay there, as being too much for the limits of a letter, especially as the boat is expected to put off immediately.

Extract of a Letter from Plymouth, May 3, 1778[1]

Arrived the Earl Bathurst armed ship in six weeks from New York, where every thing remained quiet. The Bathurst has retaken a brig with fruit, called the Betsey, a prize to Cunningham.

[1] From the London Chronicle for 1778, May 5–7.

[BRD. DEHEZ TO GUSTAVUS CONYNGHAM[1]]

(Translation)

May 18, 1778.

Mr. Gustavus Conyngham at St. Sebastian,
Sir:

Some one has assured me that you are actually at Cadiz; I am addressing the present letter to my friend, Mr. John Walmsley, of the said town. The friend in question and myself are very impatient to become acquainted with your good news. Your business is in very good order, and we will do all that is possible in order to turn it to your favor and advantage, and we hope to succeed. If you desire the welfare of your interests, give us a pledge by Mr. Larralde or Mr. Gardoquiz; they both tell me they cannot do anything without your order, and that you must give them dispensation to do it. The assessor of the cause demands that you warrant the judgment of the suit; this is a formality which it is necessary to go through, and by means of which the procedure can be put in court to be judged here or at the council of war, and without any difficulty to your advantage. The barrister you saw with me, defends the case—you could not have a better. But Captain Letournois claims upon you—and the damages you told him it occasioned, and he is not willing to leave here in spite of the fact that some one has informed him, on your behalf, that he could go away having his power of attorney, but about this will say nothing, it will be without doubt rejected from the claim; and we will do our best to put everything in your favor, as has

---

[1] MSS. in the collection of Mr. James Barnes.

been done up to . . . but it is absolutely necessary that you immediately give security, without losing a moment. You know, my dear sir, that the friend in question did this on your word of honor and upon the assurance that you would be guarantee for all emergencies, and that upon this promise he delivered to you your crew from prison, so you must not refuse it for a moment, I implore you. I wrote to Messrs. de Lagoanere of Corona about this, they defend themselves saying that they have neither your signature nor power from you. However, Mr. Macmahon wrote me on your behalf that he would do all that is necessary in the matter, you are not thus left in a scrape, and may be upon that view the orders that you have from Congress, that you risk nothing. On the contrary you would put your business in a right condition, and bring it about so that it can be heard in a Court of Justice just as well as in the Council of War.— The minister, after several pleadings having ordered to decide who should act in your defence, and allegations; to hear all parties here in a Court of Justice; and to . . . that your friends will not give bail without consenting to take charge of your interests. It would be a very unhappy thing for you, and for us, if this business turns out badly through any fault of yours and theirs. And I will not believe that you will break your word to us nor your honourable sentiments, which I believe will always accompany your signal renown and wide reputation; and if you should forfeit it the judicial order of Pecheroit would arrest you anywhere,—perhaps in France, perhaps in Spain—of your goods and person. So sir, do what is right, and be more than persuaded that we will defend you so that you will come out victorious and give you what you desire—the contrary is impossible. Be kind enough then to answer me, and write to Messrs. Gardoquiz of Bilbao, by the return of the courier; this I should see with the greatest pleasure, for the desire we have here is to oblige you, and upon that you can count.

I have the honor to be always at your service, and with the most distinguished and perfect consideration, sir, Your humble and obedient servant

BRD. DEHEZ.

[THE AMERICAN COMMISSIONERS TO GUSTAVUS CONYNGHAM[1]]

Sir, [No date]

The interest which the public has in the vessel you command, makes us regard her as a Continental ship of war. Mr. Hodge and Mr. Ross have heretofore no right to direct or control you, neither had Mr. Deane alone any right to dispose of the prizes you made, as Mnsr. Lagonere informs us he has done. You will give us an account for the future of your plans and proceedings; and the individuals who may be concerned in her, —for we know not who they are, nor how far they may have contributed,—will have their share when they prove their right.

Letters of Introduction Given to Gustavus Conyngham by Lagoanere & Co.[2]

(Translation)

Gentlemen: La Corogne, May 22, 1778.

Our friend Mr. Gustavus Conyngham commanding the war cutter The Revenge, belonging to the thirteen

[1] Draft of a letter printed in Hale's Franklin in France, Vol. I, p. 342. [2] MSS. in the collection of Mr. James Barnes.

United Colonies of North America, having asked us for a letter of credit, in order to procure the money he would want for his individual account, we have given him the present letter, which he has signed with ourselves, and which he will return to you if he makes use of it. In this case we ask you to render to him or to have rendered all the attentions which will depend on you, and to charge him or have charged all the money he will ask of you, upon drafts on us directly or payable in Madrid forty to sixty days from date. That we will collect with promptitude, we ask you to be convinced. We pray you to receive likewise our gratitude for all that you will do in favor of our recommendation and that you will always find us disposed to give you similar proofs on all other occasions.

We have the honor to be very sincerely,

Your very humble and very obedient servants

LAGOANERE & COMPY.

G. Conyngham.

Messrs. Francois Aguirre & Comp. at Nantes

M. Dome. Cabarras Jr. at Bordeaux.

MM. Robert Brothers at La Rochelle.

M. De Cabarras Sr. at Bayonne.

Mr. Ante. Betbeder at St. Sebastien.

M. Martin Dibiry at Bilbao.

M. Ante. Delmaro at St. Ander.

M. Pre. Lapeire at Vigo.

MM. Lassore Brothers and Comp. at Cadiz.

MM. J. Bape. famin Devoire & Comp. at Barcelona.

MM. Roux Brothers at Marseille.

MM. Cassalon & Comp. at Canaries Ste. Croix de Teneriffe.

On board Sloop Revenge
the 31st May 1778

Whereas on this day we fell in with the Swedish Brig America Sophia laden with British goods from London to Teneriff, & whereas Capt. Cunningham says that he has directions not to Trouble any Neutral Vessel yet the Cargo appearing to belain to the British property we have engaged him to take her, & try her chances to America

Matthew Lawler
Benjamin Peet
Patrick Pearse
Josiah Smith
Thomas Pearse
Richard McCarthy
James Duggan
W. Dalton
Mos. Hanton
Dr Lee
George Brown
Hugh Carmon
Philip Singleton
William Latimore
James Waile
John Mason
James McKorley
John Lewis
James Harvey
John Downey
Thomas Quigley

Francis Burano
James Fogarty
John X Driver
        Mark
John Kelleger

Attestation by the Crew of the Revenge,
May 31, 1778

Attestation by the Crew of the Revenge[1]

On board Sloop Revenge
the 31st May 1778

Whereas on this day we fell in with the Swedish Brigg Henerica Sophia[2] Laden with British Goods from London to Tenerif & whereas Captn. Cunningham says that he has directions not to Insult any Neuteral Flag yet, the Cargoe appearing so plain to be British property we have eng'd him to take her, & try her chance to America

Matthew Lawler[3]	William Latimore
Benjamin Peel[4]	James Naile
Patrick Hease	John Mason
Josiah Smith[5]	James Mc.Cartey
Thomas Hease	John Lewis
Richard Mc.Carthy	James Harvey
James Duggan	John Downey
W. Scallon	Thomas Grayling
Mattw. Stanton	Franceso Persano
Dr. Lee	James Fogarty
George Brown	his
Hugh Cannon	John × Driver
Philip Singelton	mark

John Thayer

[1] MSS. in the collection of Mr. James Barnes.   [2] See p. 138.
[3] First lieutenant of the Revenge.
[4] One of the Revenge's officers.   [5] Surgeon of the Revenge.

[LAGOANERE & CO. TO MR. BOUTIN, MERCHANT[1]]

(Translation)   La Corogne August 31, 1778.

Mr. F. Boutin at St. Pierre Martinique.
Sir:

Mr. Benjamin Peel officer of the armed cutter named The Revenge, belonging to the United States of North America, commanded by Mr. Gustavus Conyngham, having remitted to us a sum of five hundred and ten piastres, has asked us to give him a letter of credit of this amount on your town, we have taken the liberty to give him the present letter for you, Sir, and we ask you in consequence to be willing to charge him—the said Mr. Peel—the aforesaid sum of two thousand five hundred and fifty livres to a farthing, and to take your repayment for our said account in your agreement of one hundred days at sight upon our friend Mr. Dque. Cabarras Jr. of Bordeaux, who will there do all that is necessary for our said account, referring us to the surplus, to which we have the honor to point out to you in our letter of recommendation and credit which we have given to Captain Conyngham who is the bearer of it and which we confirm in all its contents.

We have the honor to be with great consideration, sir,
Your very humble and very obedient servants,

LAGOANERE & COMP.

[1] MSS. in the collection of Mr. James Barnes.

[LAGOANERE & CO. TO MR. BOUTIN, MERCHANT[1]]

(Translation)   La Corogne, August 31, 1778.

Mr. F. Boutin at St. Pierre, Martinique.
Sir:

Mr. Mathew Lawler, officer of the armed cutter named The Revenge, belonging to the United States of North America, commanded by Mr. Gustavus Conyngham, having remitted to us a sum of six hundred piastres, asked us to give him a letter of credit for this amount on your town, we have taken the liberty to give him the present letter for you, Sir, and we ask you in consequence to be willing to charge to him the aforesaid sum of *three thousand* livres to a farthing, and to take repayment upon our said charge at one hundred days on sight on Mr. Dque. Cabarras Jr. Merchant at Bordeaux, who will there do all that is necessary for our said charge, referring us to the surplus, which we have the honor to point out to you in the letter of recommendation and credit we have given to Captain Conyngham, who is the bearer of it and which we confirm in all its contents.

We have the honor to be with great consideration, sir,
Your very humble and obedient servants
LAGOANERE & COMP.

[1] MSS. in the collection of Mr. James Barnes.

[LAGOANERE & CO. TO F. BOUTIN[1]]

(Translation) La Corogne, August 31, 1778.

Mr. F. Boutin at St. Pierre, Martinique.

Sir:

Our friend Mr. Gustavus Conyngham, commander of the bilander or armed cutter The Revenge, belonging to the United States of North America, having asked us for a letter of credit in order to procure money for which he seems to be in want for his personal account, we have given him the present letter which he has signed with ourselves, and which he will bring to you if he makes use of it; in that case we ask you to render him or have rendered to him all the duties which will rest with you, and to charge him or charge our account with the amount of eight or nine thousand livres to a farthing, upon these receipts in triplicate take reimbursement from the sum you will give him at one hundred days on sight p_c^n upon Mr. Dque. Cabarras Jr., merchant at Bordeaux, who will honor your negotiations for the said amount.

We are informing the said Mr. Cabarras Jr., of this matter, so you can count upon his promptness in negotiating your draft and we pray you to give it your consideration or do it for any other house in your town with which he could be put in correspondence.

We have also given under date of to-day two other letters of credit upon you, sir, one for two thousand five

---

[1] MSS. in the collection of Mr. James Barnes.

hundred and fifty livres to a farthing, in favor of Mr. Benjamin Peel and the other for three thousand livres to a farthing in favor of Mr. Mathew Lawler, both officers on board with the said Mr. Conyngham, who will certify to you the identity of their persons and their signature when he makes use of these letters; and ask you at once to take your reimbursement upon Mr. Dque. Cabarras junior at one hundred days on sight $p\frac{n}{c}$, having also informed the said gentleman of it.

Our Mr. Lagoanere, head of our house established in this town nine years, has given us your address, and it is with his knowledge that we are writing you, offering you our services for you and your friends. Our Mr. Lagoanere also profits on this occasion in the renewal of your remembrance, as well as in that of madame your wife, his cousin, and asks that you both accept a thousand expressions of good will on his part. For you, we conclude, by asking you to be assured that on any other occasion you will find us always ready to prove to you the sincerity of the sentiments with which we have the honor to be, sir,

Your very humble and obedient servants,

LAGOANERE & COMPY.

G. Conyngham[1]

---

[1] Signature.

[COMTE DE CREUTZ TO THE COMTE DE VERGENNES[1]]

(Translation)
    M. de Rayneval
    1778 October 1.

Memorandum

The undersigned, Ambassador Extraordinary of His Swedish Majesty to His Most Christian Majesty, has the honour to communicate to His Excellency Count de Vergennes, Minister and Secretary of State for Foreign Affairs, an event of which he has just been informed, and which obliges him to claim the good offices of His Most Christian Majesty.

A Swedish merchant vessel named Henrica Sophia, Captain Peter Heldt, laden at London, for a Spanish house, with bales of cloth and other similar merchandise destined for Teneriffe, left London on the 9th. May last to proceed to its destination.

On the 31st. of the same month it met on the high seas an American corsair named Cunningham, who seized it and sent the ship, with the captain and three men of the crew, to America. The rest of the crew, consisting of seven men with the pilot were transferred on board the privateer, put at the bottom of the hold as prisoners, and made to experience all sorts of hardships.

He at last, at the end of three months, put into port at Corunna, where these unfortunate men found means to apply to the Dutch consul, who took an interest in them and procured their liberty.

The undersigned has no need to point out to His Excellency the utter irregularity of this proceeding. But

---

[1] Stevens's Facsimiles, Vol. XXIII, No. 1967–1, 2.

as Sweden has no relations with the United States of America, he confidently addresses himself, as the Ambassador of a King who is the friend and ally of France, to His Excellency, to beg him to be good enough, by his intervention, not only to obtain the restitution of that vessel and its cargo, with all suitable damages, but also to cause that corsair to be punished exemplarily, showing the said State the indispensable necessity for them to observe the law of nations and respect the flag of neutral powers. LE COMTE DE CREUTZ

Paris, 1st October 1778.

[COMTE DE VERGENNES TO THE COMTE DE CREUTZ[1]]

(Translation) Versailles, 6th. October 1778.

His Excellency M. le Comte de Creutz.

Monsieur,

Impossibility of granting our good offices for the restitution of a Swedish vessel taken by an American corsair.

I have received the memorandum which your Excellency did me the honour to address to me on the 1st. instant concerning the Swedish vessel seized by an American corsair called Cunningham. The King would have had pleasure in intervening with his good offices in order to procure the restitution of that vessel, but he has no right to make representations on this subject to the United States of North America, and still less to influence their principles and their conduct towards Powers which have not only no treaty with them, but which have not yet even recognized their independence.

·/.

[1] Stevens's Facsimiles, Vol. XXIII, No. 1969.

Examination of William Carmichael before Congress[1]

Monday, October 5, 1778.

Q. Are you sure that the public had any share in those two vessels which were purchased in the Mediterranean?

A. I apprehended at the time that they had, and my reason for apprehending was, that the Captain had a Continental commission; I thought they were on the same footing as those fitted out at Dunkirk.

Q. Were you anywise concerned in equipping Capt. Conyngham from Dunkirk?

A. I was in no way concerned in the equipment. I was sent by Mr. Franklin and Mr. Deane to facilitate the departure of that vessel from the port.

Q. Was Captain Conyngham's vessel fitted out at Dunkirk more than once?

A. Captain Conyngham commanded two vessels from that port, one a lugger, the other a cutter.

Q. Were they fitted at the same time?

A. At different times.

Q. Were they or either of them public or private property?

A. I apprehended that each of them were part public and part private, but I do not certainly know.

Q. When you were sent to dispatch these vessels, did

[1] In The Deane Papers, Collections of the New-York Historical Society, Vol. II, p. 497.

you consider yourself as acting for the public or for private persons?

A. Every service I performed for the Commissioners I considered as done for the public, and so I considered in this instance.

Q. What reason had you to consider these vessels as part private property?

A. From conversations I had at the time, particularly with Mr. Hodge, I had reason to apprehend he was concerned.

Q. Had you reason to suppose that Mr. Deane was concerned, or any of the Commissioners?

A. I did apprehend at that time that Mr. Deane was concerned in the first equipment.

Q. What reasons induced you to apprehend that Mr. Deane was concerned in the first equipment?

A. I cannot recollect the reasons that induced that belief, but I know that I did at the time apprehend he was concerned.

Q. At what time was the first equipment made, what year, and what month?

A. At present I cannot precisely recollect. I think it was in the spring, 1777. The captain of the Harwich packet will nearly point out the time of the sailing.

Q. Do you know if any and what instructions were given to Captain Conyngham respecting that cruise?

A. I think there were instructions given, but I cannot be particular what those instructions were.

Q. By Mr. Lee. Do you know that the vessels, or either of them, were ordered to cruise on the coast of England?

A. I speak to the first vessel. I beleive the object was

to cruise for one of the Harwich packets. I myself gave directions.

Q. Was this equipment at Dunkirk made with or without the knowledge of the French ministry?

A. I cannot answer as to the knowledge of the French ministry.

Q. Did you overhear that the French ministry objected to it?

A. I know they gave proofs that it did not appear to be agreeable, for the Captain was imprisoned upon his return to Dunkirk.

Q. Did you hear that the French ministry objected previous to the sailing?

A. I do not know that they knew of the first vessel previous to her sailing, therefore they could not object to the equipment.

Q. Did you ever hear that the French ministry offered to pay the expense of equipping those vessels, or either of them, to prevent their sailing?

A. Of the first vessel I never heard that they did; of the second, I heard after she had sailed that they had given orders to pay the expense to prevent her sailing.

Q. Did you understand that much diligence was used to push these vessels, or either of them, out of Dunkirk, to prevent the effect of the measures the ministry had taken to stop their sailing?

A. With respect to the last, I believe all possible diligence was used to accelerate her departure, to prevent measures from being taken by the ministry to stop her sailing.

Q. Did you ever see or hear of a letter or letters

written by the Count de Vergennes to M. Grand, or the Commissioners, complaining of this measure?

A. I have heard that there was such a letter, but I do not know whether to M. Grand or the Commissioners.

Q. Do you know whether the Commissioners had received any orders from Congress or the Secret Committee relative to the fitting out of these two vessels?

A. I do not know whether they had received orders relative to the fitting out of these two vessels.

Q. Did you ever hear that they had?

A. I never heard that they had received orders to fit out these two vessels particularly. I heard that they had general orders to fit out vessels.

Q. Do you mean vessels of force to cruise against the enemy?

A. I do, because they received Continental commissions for the Captains.

[SILAS DEANE TO THE PRESIDENT[1] OF CONGRESS[2]]

(Extracts)   Philadelphia, 12th October, 1778

Mr. Hodge went to Dunkirk by order of the commissioners. They sent him in consequence of orders from the Secret Committee; he purchased and fitted out two vessels, a fact, though forgotten by Mr. Lee, known to everyone at the time. From what that brave and vir-

[1] Henry Laurens.
[2] In The Deane Papers, Collections of the New-York Historical Society, Vol. III, pp. 18, 21.

tuous young American did and suffered on the occasion, it was the common topic of conversation every where; it raised insurance in England ten per cent for a time. Mr. Hodge to appease the British Ambassador, was sent to the Bastile, and Cunningham, making his cruise around England and Ireland, put into Spain without prize money equal to the repairs he wanted. Mr. Hodge was released from his imprisonment, and one of the first things he did was to give Mr. Lee the account of his whole disbursements in writing. Mr. Hodge had taken a small interest in the adventure from the first, and proposed following Cunningham into Spain by land, and making a cruise with him. He proposed that Mr. Ross and he should purchase the vessel; but as a price could not easily be agreed upon, they proposed to take the vessel as she was, and do the best with her against the common enemy, and to account to Congress therefor. Mr. Ross desired that such an agreement should be signed by the commissioners for his security. I know not that it was ever done. I have only to add on this subject, that all the monies received by Mr. Hodge amounted to 92,729 livres 18.3 in the whole, and that Mr. Hodge rendered us other services besides equipping these two vessels.

.   .   .   .   .   .

Having forgot to mention it in its place, I must be permitted to add here, that the first vessel purchased and fitted out by Mr. Hodge was, on the return and imprisonment of Cunningham, detained by order from Court, and a second purchased, in which Cunningham went on his second cruise. The first was put up for sale at Dunkirk, but not disposed of when I left Paris, at least I had not heard of it.

*Extract from Silas Deane's Narrative, Read
before Congress*[1]

From Dunkirk, Mr. Hodge fitted out Captain
Conyngham in a cutter, with the design of intercepting
a rich packet-boat from Harwich, to destroy some of the
transports carrying over the Hessian troops to England,
and to cruise in the Northern Ocean. Captain Conyngham captured a packet-boat, and supposing he had intercepted important intelligence, unadvisedly returned
into port. He also took a brig on his return. Mr.
Hodge came up to Paris with the letters taken in the
packet. Orders were sent from the court to restore the
two prizes, to detain Captain Conyngham's vessel, and
to imprison him and his people. These orders were
executed; but these expeditions caused a great sensation
to the British commerce; and for the first time since
Britain was a maritime power, the River Thames and
other of its ports were crowded with French and other
ships taking in freight, in order to avoid the risk of having British property captured.

After the alarm had a little subsided, liberty was
obtained to send Captain Conyngham and his people
out of France, in another vessel. To effect this, Mr.
Carmichael went with Mr. Hodge to Dunkirk, purchased and fitted out a second vessel well armed against
the insults of British cruisers, and ordered Captain
Conyngham not to cruise or commit hostilities on the
coast of France. Captain Conyngham sailed with the

[1] In The Deane Papers, Collections of the New-York Historical
Society, Vol. III, p. 167.

resolution of following his orders, but he had not been long at sea before his people mutinied and obliged him to make prizes. This renewed the alarm in England, occasioned fresh and warm complaints from that side; to silence which, Mr. Hodge was confined in the Bastile for five or six weeks, where he was treated as well as a prisoner could be, and suffered in nothing but the confinement, which indeed was sufficiently severe to one of his spirit and feelings.

Captain Conyngham pursued his cruise, sailed round England and Ireland, and carried a prize with him into Spain, which, from the then situation of affairs there, turned to little account, as did also some others he afterwards captured.

[BENJAMIN FRANKLIN TO FERDINAND GRAND[1][2]]

Sir: Passy, October 14, 1778.

I have considered the note you put into my hands containing a complaint of the conduct of Captain Conyngham in the Revenge privateer. We have no desire to justify him in any irregularities he may have committed. On the contrary, we are obliged to our friends who give us information of the misconduct of any

[1] A French Protestant from Switzerland, who through influence obtained the reputation and emolument of being banker to the American Ministers; his brother, Sir George Grand, was in partnership with a banking house in Amsterdam and enjoyed the favor and confidence of the French Ministers of State.

[2] MSS. Department of State; printed in Wharton's Diplomatic Correspondence of the American Revolution, Vol. II, p. 784.

cruisers, that we may take the occasion of representing the same to our Government, and recommending more effectual provisions for suppressing, punishing, and preventing such practices in future.

By the papers I have the honor to send you enclosed, and which I request you would put into the hands of his excellency Count of Aranda, the care of the Congress, to avoid giving offense to neutral powers will appear most evident: First, in the commission given to privateers, wherein it appears that sureties are taken of their owners that nothing shall be done by them "inconsistent with the usage and custom of nations," and those sureties are obliged to make good all damages. Courts of admiralty are regularly established in every one of the United States for judging of such matters, to which courts any person injured may apply, and will certainly find redress. Secondly, in the proclamation of Congress, whereby strict orders are given to all officers of armed vessels to pay a sacred regard to the rights of neutral powers and the usage and customs of civilized nations, and a declaration made that if they transgress they shall not be allowed to claim the protection of the States, but shall suffer such punishment as by the usage and custom of nations may be inflicted on them. Lastly, in the particular care taken by Congress to secure the property of some subjects of Portugal (a power that has not been very favorable to us), although no reclamation has been made.

All these will show that the States give no countenance to acts of piracy; and if Captain Conyngham has been guilty of that crime he will certainly be punished for it when duly prosecuted, for not only a regard to justice in general, but a strong disposition to cultivate the friendship of Spain, for whose sovereign they have the greatest respect, will induce the Congress to pay great attention to every complaint, public and private, that shall come from thence.

I have, etc., B. FRANKLIN.

[BENJAMIN FRANKLIN TO FERDINAND GRAND[1]]

Passy, November 3, 1778.

We owe our thanks, sir, to the person who has transmitted to us, through you, the complaint we have received against Mr. Conyngham, and we can assure him anew that penetrated with respect for S. M. C., nothing pains us more than complaints on his part against our people. He will have seen, by the papers transmitted by you at the time from us to S. E. M., Count d'Aranda, the measures which Congress have taken to prevent any misconduct on the part of our privateers and seamen, and nothing better proves its solicitude in this regard than the proclamation it has just issued, of which the enclosed No. 2 is a copy, and to which we join its resolution for the protection of the property of a ship although belonging to a power with which we have no sympathy.

But if one directs his attention to the atrocious pro-

[1] MSS. Department of State; printed in Wharton's Diplomatic Correspondence of the American Revolution, Vol. II, pp. 827–828; translated from a French version transmitted by Count d'Aranda to Florida Blanca and now deposited in the Archivo General de Reino in Simancas. In the correspondence between Grantham (British Minister at Madrid) and Weymouth (Secretary of State), the exploits of Conyngham are constant topics of discussion.

ceedings of the English towards all nations without distinction, he will not be surprised that their pernicious example finds imitators among some individuals of a nation which they have so greatly outraged. But this does not excuse Conyngham. It is a crime in our eyes to have displeased a power for which Congress is penetrated with respect, and although justified in seizing, by way of reprisals, the English prize which Conyngham had brought to Teneriffe to be sent to Martinique, we will none the less inform Congress of the grounds for complaint which this privateer has given to his catholic majesty. This will certainly be a new motive for paying to his flag the homage and respect which it entertains for him. I hope from the wisdom as well as from the justice of S. M. that he will confide in this expression of our sentiments towards him and in turn will permit us to experience the effects of them.

I have, etc.,

B. FRANKLIN.

[ARTHUR LEE TO THE COMMITTEE OF
FOREIGN AFFAIRS[1]]

(Extract)   Paris, November 15, 1778.

I am informed that a Swedish ship, the Henrica Sofia, Captain P. Held, loaded with Spanish property, bound from London to Teneriffe, has been taken by Captain Cunningham in the Revenge, which, being considered in Spain as a violence done to them, has

[1] MSS. Department of State; printed in Wharton's Diplomatic Correspondence of the American Revolution, Vol. II, p. 840.

given great offense. I have assured them that, upon its being made to appear in the admiralty court in America that the property is neutral, it will be restored, with such damages as are just. The court of Spain is so much offended at Captain Cunningham's conduct before this, that they write me orders have been sent to all their ports to prohibit his entrance. From the beginning to the end of this business of Cunningham, it has been so bad, that Congress only can correct it by punishing those who are concerned. It has cost the public more than 100,000 livres, and embroiled us both with the French and Spanish courts.[1]

[WILLIAM BINGHAM[2] TO GUSTAVUS CONYNGHAM[3]]

St. Pierre M/que Novem 29th. 1778

Capt Conyngham
Sir

The Instructions which I gave you under Date of October 26 will serve to regulate your Conduct in most Cases in regard to the present Cruize.

As the defensive Alliance entered into betwixt France & the United States of America will point out to you one Common Object as the Motive that our Conduct is mutually to be regulated by, that of annoying & circumventing the Designs of the Enemy, I must seriously recommend to you not to lose sight of it—And

---

[1] This, so far as concerns France, was a mistake. The displeasure of the French Minister with Conyngham was only put on to save appearances. See Deane to Morris, August 23, 1777; the Commissioners to the Committee, May 25, 1777.

[2] The Continental agent at St. Pierre, Martinique.

[3] MSS. in the collection of Mr. James Barnes.

as it is certain that the Count D'Estaing has taken his Departure from America bound for this Place, I beg that you would studiously endeavor to deliver the inclosed Letter to him, as it is of very material Importance.

Accounts have been received this Day of the sailing of a Frigate with Transports under her Convoy & a great Number of Troops from France;—If you should fall in with this Fleet you will take Care to advise the Captain of the Frigate that Admiral Barrington has fixed his Cruizing Ground to the windward of this Island, that he may take Care to avoid falling into the Hands of the Enemy—

Another grand Object that must attract your Attention is the endeavouring to capture some of the Transports that have sailed from Newport bound for the English West India Islands— It appears that they have suffered by a Gale of Wind & have lost their Convoy, so that perhaps they will fall an easy Prey—

No Recompence could requite the services you would render your Country by capturing some of those that have Troops on board, as it might perhaps hinder the success of their Operations in these Seas—

With wishing you a pleasant & successfull Cruize I remain with great Regard

Sir　Your obed hble Servt
Wm Bingham

PS—I herewith enclose you the Signals that you are to make if you should fall in with any Fleet that you may suppose to be that of the Count D'Estaing—As they are in French you will take Care to have them interpreted by those such Persons on board that you may repose unlimited Confidence in—

Extract from the Journals of Congress,
Dec. 26, 1778[1]

A memorial from Josiah Smith, surgeon, and others, late of the Revenge cutter, Captain Cunningham, was read:

Ordered, That it be referred to the Marine Committee.

Report of the Marine Committee, Jan. 4, 1779[2]

The Marine Committee to whom was referred the Memorial of Josiah Smith, Surgeon, and others late of the Revenge Cutter Captain Cuningham, beg leave to report as their Opinion. That Captain Cuningham the Commander of said Cutter be directed forthwith to repair to this City or any other place where Congress may be sitting and render an account of his conduct during his command of the said Cutter, in pursuance of complaints exhibited against him by divers of his officers and crew.

January 4th 1779

[1] In Journals of the Continental Congress (Lib. of Cong. Edit.), Vol. XII, p. 1256.
[2] Papers of the Continental Congress, No. 37, folio 165; printed in Journals of the Continental Congress, Vol. XIII, p. 25.

Account of Prizes taken in the Surprize by Capt. Gustavus Conyngham.[1]

Date When Taken	Names of Prizes	Guns	Men	Cargo	Whole Value	Ports Where Sent	Agents in Those Ports	Occasional Notes
1777 May 3d	Harwich Packet			Wine fruit Oil Raw silk	£5000 Sterlg	Dunkirque	Morrill, Murdock Hodge & Coffin ditto	{Forced into Dunkirque by contrary Winds & English {Cruizers & deld up by order of the Court of France Ditto German Ocean
" 4th	Brig Joseph			do.	£1500 Stlg	do.		{Taken in the German Ocean & there burnt {in Sight of an English Ship of War
						In the Revenge		
July 21	Schoon Happy Return			Tea, Gin & Brandy Cordials	£20,000 Stlg	Dunkirque		{Taken in the same Ocean & there burn't as it was {impossible to get her in for English Cruizers
" 23d	Brig Maria			Ballast	£2500 Stlg	Do.		Taken in same Ocean & ransom'd for above Reasons
" 25	Brig Patty				Ransom'd for £650 Stlg			
" 26	Brig Northampton			Hemp & Iron		Ordered to France for Spain		Carried to England by Bayley Prizemaster
From 26 July 1777 to 10 March 1778.	Brig Venus			Whale Oil Wine Oil Fruit & in part of wine & dry Cod fish	Rls. 23.13.6 80,000 Rls. 187,518	Hull	Ferroll Lagoncire & Co.	Retaken off Barbados do. channel Retaken off Barbados sent to Bayone under direction of Mr. Lagoncire (taken in Bay of Biscay)
	Brig Black Prince						Coruna Do.	ditto. (off Oporto)
	Brig Brothers		4				Do.	ditto. (off Cape Finnister)
	Ship Two Brothers		10	Goods & Ballast	Rls. 19,420 (Hull 10,684 Cargo)			
	Brig Graciosa			Dry Goods				
	Ship Hope		6	Fish	S Revenges 7/8 each part is Rls. 145,670	St. Sebastian's Bilboa	Gardoqui & Co. ditto	sent for Bilboa (by distress of Weather St. Sebastians) & there given up by order of Court of Spain (taken off Cape Ortugal) Arrived. taken in Bay of Biscay
March 11	Brig Peace & Harmony		15	Fruit		Newbury Port	Tracey	Prize Master Squire carrd to Nantucket & sold her (taken in the Atlantic)
12	Brig Betsey			Barilla			do.	retaken on the Coast of America ('Taken in the Atlantic)
13	Snow Fanny		8	Fruit & Wine	Lrs. 32,675.17.0		do.	(On Coast of Portugal, arrived at Martinique & sold by
20	Enterprize Kings Tender		6			Do.		(D H Conyngham & paid into the hands of Mr Bingham.
24	Ship Hope		16	Fruit & Raw Silk	£2000 Stlg	Do.		Taken off Cape St. Vincents & there burn'd on acct. of an English Frigate.
April 19	Brig Carbonere		25	Salt	Rls 100,000	Do.	Lacouta & Co.	Taken off the Straights mouth & retaken by the Enterprize Frigate
16	Brig Tapley		10	Butter & Ballast		Cadiz		(ditto) carried by Prize master Hornsby to Halifax
19	Brig Countess of Mouton		4	Fruit & Wine	Lrs 40,947.9.8	Newbury Port	taken Sn. Mouth	(ditto) & Arrived.
May 4	Brig Maria		6			Do.	Lagoneire & Co	Arrived at Martinique sold by D H Conyngham & the Amot. paid into the hands of Mr Bingham
19	Brig Maria		15	Porter cheese & dry Fish	Coruna			Off Cape Finnister—Arrived
	Brig Dispatch			dry goods	rls 81,080	Do.	Do.	Bay of Biscay.
	Brig Siren			dry Fish		Do.	Do.	Ditto. do. at Ferroll.
31 do.	Honora Sophia			Ditto		Newbury Port	W. Bingham	Off Cape Finnister, retaken of Cape Codd
	Sloop Two Friends			Ballast		Martinico	Curson & Governus Ditto.	Off St Eustatia, retaken
Novr.	Two Schooners		37	Privateer	Lrs 6,270	St Eustatia	W. Bingham	& there ransomed
Novr.	Schooner Adml. Barrington	6 G. 14 S.	59	Ditto	Lrs 19,500	Martinico	Do.	Ditto. Arrived
Novr.	Brig Loyalist	10 G. 14 S.		Ditto	Lrs 6650	Do.	Do.	Windwd. St. Martins do.
	Brig Suckey			Ballast	Lrs 2000	Do.	Do.	Off Antigua. do.
		66	197					

[1] MSS. in the collection of Mr. James Barnes. Rls. stands for reales (Spanish); Lrs. for livres (French); £, for pounds sterling (English).

[WILLIAM BINGHAM TO GUSTAVUS CONYNGHAM[1]]

I do require you as an Officer in the Service of the Congress to repair on board the Danish Brig, captured by an American Privateer & seal down the Hatches of said Vessel, her Cargoe appearing to be the property of the Subjects of the King of Portugal, that Justice may be duly administered in the Case. And for so doing, this shall be your sufficient warrant.

Given under my Hand, this sixteenth Day of January, in the year of our Lord 1779.

To   WM. BINGHAM

   Gustavus Conyngham,
      Commander of the Continental
      armed Cutter, the Revenge.

Extract from the Boston Gazette, February 15, 1779

ST. PEIRRE, (Martinico) Dec. 10.

The American vessel the Revenge of 18 guns, commanded by the brave Cunningham, arrived here from Corunna, which he left on the 1st of September. This intrepid Commander, so well known for his having taken an English Packet-boat, and by that a Cutter of 18 guns, having spread terror through the coasts of Eng-

---

[1] MSS. in the collection of Mr. James Barnes.

[153]

land, Scotland and Ireland, carried his flag with the same success to the Mediterranean. In 18 month's cruize, he has taken 27 English vessels, and sent them into different ports, and has sunk or burnt 33.

Dec. 20. The American cruizer the Revenge, commanded by the celebrated Cunningham, is returned from her cruize, bringing with her an English brig, the Loyalist, Capt. Morris, of 12 guns, and the sloop Admiral Barrington, Capt. Pelham, of 8 guns. He has taken besides another vessel which he has sent to Guadaloop; and two small sloops which he ransomed. He had an engagement off Barbadoes with a King's Cutter of 28 guns, which he pursued near the guns of the fort, and which would not have escaped, had it not been for an high sea which prevented his boarding her.

Extract from the Journals of Congress,
February 22, 1779[1]

The Committee of Commerce communicated to Congress a letter from W. Bingham, by which it appears that he has shipped on board the Revenge, cutter, 50 chests of arms:

Ordered, That the Board of War give directions to have the arms which are arrived in the Revenge, cutter, Captain Cunningham, examined and send by the safest and most speedy conveyance to South Carolina such of them as are fit for service.

[1] In Journals of the Continental Congress, Vol. XIII, p. 236.

[RICHARD PETERS TO GUSTAVUS CONYNGHAM[1]]

Sir   War Office Feby. 24. 1779

Please to deliver to the Order of Col. Benjamin Flower Commisary General of Military Stores Fifty Chests of Arms the Property of the United States imported in the Revenge Cutter from Martinique & consigned to the Hon: the Marine Committee by whom they were delivered over to this Board.

I am your very obed Servt

RICHARD PETERS

By Order & in Behalf of the Board.

Capt. Cunningham
Officer Comanding the Revenge Cutter
Philadelphia.

[THE MARINE COMMITTEE TO MESSRS. JACKSON,
TRACEY & TRACEY[2] [3]]

March 10th. 1779.

Messrs. Jackson, Tracey, & Tracey
Gentlemen

This Committee have very important public reasons for developing with great certainty and exactness, the origin, progress and designs of Captain Conyngham and the Cutter he commanded called the Revenge. By Captain Conyngham's narrative it appears to the Committee that many Prizes taken by him have been ad-

[1] MSS. in the collection of Mr. James Barnes.
[2] Probably an American commercial house.
[3] Marine Committee Letter-book, p. 201.

dressed to your House, in consequence of which the Committee request of you Gentlemen that you will send them by the next post after you receive this an account of what Prizes have arrived to your address from Captain Conyngham, and for what and how they have been disposed. And also a Copy of all the Instructions you may have received from any person whatever concerning such Prizes. The honorable mention that has been made of you Gentlemen to the Committee, induces me to believe that you will excuse the trouble that may arise from furnishing the particular account above desired, as the public business demands it.

I have the honor to be Gentlemen
Your very hble servant
RICHARD H. LEE *Chairman*

[THE MARINE COMMITTEE TO JOSEPH REED[1]]

March 12th 1779

His Excellency Joseph Reed Esqr
    President of Pennsylvania
Sir

I have the honor to inform your Excellency that upon a full consideration of the complicated affairs of the Cutter Revenge it has been thought proper and it is determined by Congress that the Vessel with her Guns, Apperal &c shall be sold at Public Auction and the

---

[1] Marine Committee Letter-book, p. 201.

Marine Committee has derected that the sale shall be
made at the Coffee House in this City next wedensday
evening.

> I have the Honor to be
> Your Excellencys Hble Servant
> RICHD. HENRY LEE *Chairman*

[THE BOARD OF WAR TO GUSTAVUS CONYNGHAM[1]]

> Marine Office
> March 17th 1779

Sir

The Marine Committee desire that you will deliver
to the Board of War the Piglead now on board the Cutter Revenge—taking care to ascertain the weight and
taking a receipt for what you deliver

> I am Sir
> Your Obed Servant
> per Order
> JOHN BROWN
> *Secry*

Captain Gustavus Conyngham
of the Cutter Revenge

[1] MSS. in the collection of Mr. James Barnes.

Attestation of Gustavus Conyngham[1]

1779 left martinique for AM arrived at phila Febry. 1779 shortly after the Navy board took the direction of sd. Cutter revenge & under their direction and she was solde at public sale by an act of Congress 12th. March 79. Some time after peace by an Order of Congress a commercial agent was appointed to settle every Acct. relative to the publick in Europe & did call on every house concerned with the revenge for that purpose through the agency of Willm. Carmichal at Madrid.

from the first day of the revolution my Motive was to Injure & distress the Enemy every way possible in my power some of they Commissr object was a commd. of funds, this I had no concearn with or a controul. on my accts. being presented at the Secry. of State Office, Alexd. hamilton & papers. he assured me a report should be to Congress without delay—Notwithstand every difficulty was throwed in my way of a settlement by Arthur Lee Esqr. & his influence being in Congress & the departmt of State at the time, petition after petition to Congress time after time to no effect from 1779 to decembr. 26th. 1797—the cutter purchased by individuals I applyed to the Marine board if the Commission I held was or was not sufficient to entitle me as expressed an officer in the AM Navy, should I continue in the comd. of said cutter, & they, and different members of Congress assured me it was. In consequence

[1] MSS. in the collection of Mr. James Barnes.

went on a cruize under sd. AM commss.—taken carried
to N. York, Lodged in the condemned dungeon 14 days
on a 4 penny Loaf of Bread & a little Watter, afterwards
with Irons 55 lbs. wt. sent to England by order of that
monster Sr. George Collier to be kept in the coal hole
on bread & watter for the passage. Capt. Bull comd. of
the packett had other feelings than that tyrant, Collier,
releived me from the coal pit, had he not, I must have
perished. On arrival at falmouth Lodged in pen-
dinnes Castle, further punishmt, figure of 4 hand Irons
as the sd..to be all of a piece, 120 days I suffered in dungeons on half alowance for 24 hours viz 6 oz beef &
6 of bread the worst Quallity, Committd on high
treason Act to that prison at plymout to stand trial wh.
our Gracious Good Soverng George the 3d. the Letter
of my beloved wife to Congress & the order taken on it
I refer for more information, this I new nothing of.

When removed from prison in N. York to be put on
bd. the packett, I was put in the hang-mans cart. A
Negro Called George Washington, decorattd. as usall
wh. ropes taking dezerters & others to the gallows &
executted often before us close to the prison. Attended
by a Garde of hessians, such we were often condoled wh.
during our captivity. You will go next.

NB, in the yr. 1775 I. went on a voyage from philad.
to Europe to procure powder salt-peter, arms, medecins
& every thing Necessary for War well known the Great
need & scarcity the little Supply we had at that day.
Arrived at dunkirk—here the suplys could not be procured, some part could, but we could not take any thing
in heare—a agent went to amsterdam—

Minutes from Gustavus Conyngham
of his treatment and remarks
27th Aprill 1779[1]

On the Latter end of Aprill year 79 taken by the
Galatea Capt. Jordan. On first Going A board the
ship abused by a Mr. Coaupe who acted as first Lieut.
and took my Commission. he sent everyone without ex-
ception to the hold. After some time a message came
for Capt. Conyngham; introduced to the Gun room.
Mr.   purser of the ship Mr. Thomas Surgeon
of the ship Mr. Murry Master, After some little time
Mr. Coaupe the Lieut. makes his appearance. I find
his behaviour Different to what I had reason to expect.
I am made to understand it is the Capt. Orders to be
treated well and liberty on his Quarter deck. the officers and men still in the hold Verry disagreeable so
warm, the following day Mr. Welsh my first Lieut,
Mr. Heyman 2d Lieut., Mr. Lewis Capt. of Marines,
Mr. Downey, Master, releived from the hold Liberty
of the Lower Decks. Mr. Cambel a prize master order
into Irons, by Mr. Coaupe Lieut. Mr. Coaupe spoke to
me on the subject Desired I should speak to Cambell
acknowledge his fault and should be let out of irons. I
went to Cambell Ask what he had said he declared
Mr. Coaupe Called where is that rascall or damned
scoundrell Campbell, (I do not recollect the Answer
made by Campbell) but declared he said nothing to
Give him offence, in consequence could not acknow-

---

[1] MSS. in the collection of Mr. James Barnes.

CAP.N
CUNINGHAM.

Engraved from the Original Sketch which was taken by an Artist of
Eminence, and stuck up in the English Coffee House at Dunkirk

Captain Conyngham

ledge a fault not Guilty off, some time afterwards Let
out of Irons—At our arrivall in New-York Mr. Welsh
sent on board the Commodore Sr. George Collier, &
Mr. Welsh at his return on boarde the Galetea told me
he was solicited to enter on board his ship. What an
honour to walk his majestey Quarter deck, Mr. Welsh
Declared he would not he was a prisoner on ship
Answer. he was made you shall go to england with
Mr. Conyngham & Dismisd. Soon Learned by Mr.
Coauper that my people was to be Distrubuted among
the Men of War. Boats came A Longside with officers
for the prisoners, (One officer in particular by his appearance A Lieut. an Irish man, addressed me in those
words. So Mr. Conyngham you have   Long and
in Different stages. I answered him not so many or so
long. I no better, can you be quallifyd. After some
hesitation walk. off. I do declare I never seen this person before) the crew and officers sent on board Different
Men of War, as I have understood after many threat-
nings to get them to enter the Major part was Sent on
board the prison ship with the officers. After being in
the east river Detained On board the Galetea with one
Leg in Irons I petitioned Capt. Read to alter my situation if posible to be put a long with other America Prisoners, in a short time was sent to the purvoest prison,
With officers and Guard of Marines, application made
A Deputy Serjeant or rather the turnkey A Mr. Leang
conductted me to the condemned room, where was one
person that was in on suspision of being concerned in
thieft, another supposed to be a Spy. A dismall pros-
pect. at evening the provest Master Cunningham
came to see me. I beg to know the reason of such usage.
he said his order was to put me in the strongest room

without Any person A long with me. Keept in this room one week without the least Morsel of Bread, from the Jeaoler. Watter I had give to me. Continentall prisoners found a Method through the key hole of the door to convey some Nessaries of Life through, altho a second door obstructed the Getting in very much. at the end of the week let out of this room. Introduced into the congress room by Mr. Cunningham, liberty of the prison, the 17 June Dupty Serjeant a Mr. Ghiby, Desired I should Get ready to Go on board the prison ship; After some little time Mr. Leang came to the door, calld. for me, took my leave of fellow prisoners Went down stairs; was Conveyed to another privatt apartment, then a large heavy Irons was brought with two Large Links and ring Ordered on. Limped to the Jaol door, impossible to walk Got into a cart that was provided for that purpose and led to Watter side by the hang man. took in a boat a Long side of the Commodore Sr. George Collier his ship reasonable, there I was showne an order to take me on boarde the packett in irons. Singned, Jones. to this time was made to believe Going on board the prison ship, but from every circumstance attends this place coulde expect Nothing but Deceit and falsehood.

A tale coulde be told that would if posible for the heardend rocks to hear would Melt them Asunder

G. CONYNGHAM.

At night put into Irons in a room by myselve next the Guarde house . . .

9th. In the morning taken out of Irons, room lockt up the Scentry at the door, heare I. understand the Man who keeps the Cantin is at Liberty, and the Serjeant, to fetch me what is Nessary, and the leave to Go to the Nessary, with two Sentrys, when wanted. This day Capt. Bull and Lady came to see me and very politley asked if I wantted money, or any thing, Answered No with complasance, tho at the same time could not comd. any one thing. A person, Something came to the Window asked if he had not seen me 3 months agoe in London, he declared he had he observe, that another, old acquaintance of mine was heare or words to that purpose. this Gentl. appears at the Window, I could not make my selve acquainted with, this man his behaviour apperance spoke him the gentl. Night the Irons put on.

10th. In the morning Irons took off. Nothing worthy of remarking At night Irons on.

11th. Taken out of Irons people very Curious. Nothing worthy of Notice, At Night put in Irons.

12 in the morning Irons off, the room so close confined begged to have the door oppend. Granted with having the Irons put on my Legs, Agreed too, A young man Named Deserra calld. into my room. Appd. sorry to see me in such a condition Offerd me Books to amuse me, having a person to condole with me Drew tears from me. Sodger May Sutler for the Garison bought for me a small Looking Glass, pockett Book & combe payd him ¼ the first money every payd in england. put into Irons.

13th. Irons taken off Learned from a soldier that last war being in America, and on their march from Albany, to N. York. had made a stop at kings-bridge that their officers on the march before them had returned and desired them to put up at such a house and after feingning, some pretences, to do all the mischief in their power, thiss did not require a long studdy, the furniture, soon to destruction. A number of canary birds in same manner, Complaint made to the officers: why did you give soldiers Liquor; what will soldiers not do, when drunk, it is not in our power to punish them heare, my friend. Mr. Cooper, Doctor of the packett calls to see me frequently, at 4 in the evening Irons put on, then the door left open to Give some air. I have been told the french have stopd. the dutch Mercht. Men in their ports. A young man the Name of hartshorne stopd. at my door, appeard, something dejectted. A person in Black wh. him. A woman I took to be a soldiers wife used some abusive Language to me.

14th. Nothing verry particular. Capt. Gibson called in to my room. The 2d Lieut. of a press Gang. stopd. at the steps made some curious observations. Corporal of the Guarde this day (toulson) I find a good sort of aman and well acquainted with the world, in the morning took out of Irons. at night put in, door Lockt. Verry warm & sultry. troubled with a severe head-ack. A person of the Name: Sammuel Manning, Sent me a message, that he would come to see me, only that did not like trouble, that he was well acquainted with me being mess mates and I was born in Newrey. this man I was told is above 60 year of age. Arrivd a small fleet from Irland & 4 Tenders with pressd men.

15th. In the morning Irons taken off. Weather something more cool. Not so warme been informed the english Grand fleet consisting of 30 ships of the Line sailed the 11th, and that 10 Ships of the Line had Arrived in the downs from russia, and was suspectted would joine their fleet. at night Irons put on. Door lockt.

16th. The english fleet in sight stand to the Westd.

from appearance about 35 sail of the Line,   10 sail of
frigates & fire Ships.   the person of the Name of Manning called to see me after some little time he declared
I was not that person—the Serjeant of the Guarde Mr.
Williams at the time ask this man did he meane William Cunningham Borne in thomas Street Dublin that
was taken at Stoney Batter by a Serjeant and Guarde,
that said Cunningham killed 1 Serjeant and two pri-
vates.   Afterwards the rest secured him Lodged him in
New-Gate.   Afterwards the same Conyngham was
executed in Dublin.   two Gentl. called into my room
and verry politley enquired in the Manner I was
treated.   Lord Viscount Beatmen commands the herd-
fordshire Militia in this place, this Nobleman has 2702
pounds pr. year for being Master of his Majestyes
Buck-hounds.   A person by the name McDermed Declares he New me about 10 years agoe in this place
having the Command of a schooner and that he beleived
she belonged to Virginia, that I had sent him sd. Mc.
Dermont with a message to Stephen Clear to see if he
would sceat 2 pair of Breeches for me.   A Mr. homes,
Declared he New me at St. Column in the County of
Cornwall, 4 or 5 people enquired is that the piratt. by
their appearance Country Squires or something there
abouts.   Afterwards I found this person to be an ale
keeper who pretended to know me . . . in the morning
Irons taken off, put on for the Night.

17th.   in the morning Irons taken off.   I find the
officer, thomas reckt, ensigne, who Gives and sees the
Capt. orders executted steady well disposed, if in his
                  ; this day the room close confined.   A New
Lock and hinges order for the door, the women heare
falls short of the discription I have often hearde off.

Men in common, Dark complection, not tall. Dress plain, round bottom wigs, verry fond of sticks when walking, Black their favorite coloure, pendinnis castle commanded by Capt. thomas tidd. George Lewis hamilton Lieut. at preasant under an arrest, thomas Reckt, ensigne (4 Sergeants 4 Corporals those commands a Guard of 14 men turn about that do the dutty of this place) This day so close confined could not make any observations. I find an alteration in the officer of the day and centry. in the evening Irons put on Doctor Coopper call at the window. Not liberty speak.

18th. In the morning Irons took off Dark and cloudy with small drops of rain Wind to the Southd. Capt. Dickson. born in Derry called in to my room, conversed some time, and found him acquainted with some of my friends. I have learned the people of this part of the country are so fond of tea that the Commonly buy one half-pennys worth, and make up of it without sugar, (4 people called to see me after being admitted at the door, the ask the Corporal is that Mr. Conyngham, he said no. I knew it for we well know Capt. Conyngham) A woman pretty Good appearance, verry curious to see me. Centinel would not admit of it. Many people this day and curious almost impossible for the centry to keep them from the windows. Mondays, Wednesdays, and Saturdays the post comes in heare; Monday night, Thursday and Saturday night post Goes out of this place. Irons put on.

19th. Irons took off wrote a few lines to Capt. Tidd requesting some little Liberty. Could not be grantted that his order was to keep me continually in Irons. I have obserd. that the soldiers wwho do the dutty heare, makes not any difference let who will pass—, the are mostly f—— without the least manner of notice on either side. Some little rain, at 12 cleard. up, the wind to the Westd. This day I am told that an order is come from London to keep me in Irons, booth Legs and Arms constantly at night on my Legs and my Arms Irons put.

20th. Nothing particular. Close wr. the Door admitted open. Irons on according to orders.

21st. two Gentlemen, one of them a Doctor Bonne belonging. to falmouth the other from plymouth called in to see me behav. Verry genteel. The weather cool. my room being so full of fleas it is realy a torture, to lay down, my hands confined cannot rub or scratch. I cannot rest, nor can I move with the Greattest Difficulty from place to place.

22d. fresh winds from the Westd. & rain.

23d. Do. Do. A Sailor Declared in falmouth before different people he could take his oath that I was with Capt. Jones when he threatened to set White heaven on fire. This was told me by sergeant Williams of the Guarde. On the 20th of June sailed under convoy of the Camilla for England, 45 Lg. from the hook parted convoy, On the passage applyd to the Capt. to have the Links taken off my fetters if possible not being able to move with them. After some time the Links and ring taken off, about the Banks of Newfoundland took a sloop Capt. Glover bound to some part of N. england. On the 7th of Jully arrived in falmouth harbour, the Americans taken into the press boat. 8th. the first insult recd. from a Mr. Jowlings of that place, a middling stout man, Dark Complection, Likewise from a taylor the name of Clear. A little man red eyes appearance of a worthleys man. Capt. Bull came on boarde shewed me and read his order from Sr. George Collier, the purport of it was to keep me in close confinement to be arrived in falmouth; there put me in close confiment in pendinnis Castle, to the order of the Lords was known. At about 11 o'clock put on shore, recd. by a Guard and Capt. thomas who comd. at the Castle. On the road to the Castle Manny insults and observations by the people . . . 2 Surprizing remarks, two men applyed to see me, they saying they new me. I begd of the scentry robert Beatle, to see those men, the being granted Liberty to come to the Guarde house door, one of them obserd. is that the man. Yes. I do not believe it by G—d. the other, If it is he is a rascall and D—m scoundral &c &c. this day the Irons on my hands beat close to my ribs. Lord Beatmon, Sr. John Major of the Militia and reguallitting Capt. of the press called into my room. After severall questions, Lord Beatmon verry polittley leaft the room and his Company.

24th. this day very warme and sultry. Lieut. Gayton took me from the Castle told me he was to Lodge me in mill prison, plymouth, put on board the tender fanny in falmouth harbour at night Irons put on and double centinals placed. Lodgd press room.

25th. This morning the reguallatting Capt. Bean. I apply to him to have my Irons took of my hands. Grantted. this room in the vessell is made to keep there presd. men in. Verry close, this day severe head ack. John Beach his Brother called on me to enquire after him. Lieut. John haris came on board. After some Little conversation told me I should have the same Liberty as the pressd men, while under his Comd.

26th. this is the first night Lay out of Irons since the 20th June. Lieut. haris called me & took my name on

what account I can not tell, this day have not that liberty expectted, the names of people I find wrote in the
press room R. Stuart, Andrew Miller, John Williams,
Samuel Lewis, Ritchard Nicker, Pritcher Skinner,
William Chadwell, Abraham howard, Pritchard perry,
piere hamel, Unmored their ship Lieut. haris told me
his order of so strickt. could not be admittd. on deck
without the Irons being on. I agreed to, the hold so
warme not able to endure it.

27th. This day came on boarde prisoners that was
taken belonging to the Black prince privateer prize-
master Jonathen Arnold the English fleet off the Man-
acles the wind to the Westd. Jonathen Arnold and his
crew was marched 38 miles chained two and two with
a guard of 24 men and officer charged Bayonnets peces
Loaded. A Spanish Capt. & passenger Bryan Murphy,
A Clergyman Going hom to his Native Country was
marched with 2 soldiers Drawn Cutlasses all these people was Lodged in the press room, from the peoples
Accts. was most terribly use by the Natives. No light
this night.

28th. this morning Dark and intermitting showers
of small rain Lord Beatmon and regullating Capt.
Beane came on board the priest Got his liberty,
Spanish Capt his parole. Mr. Arnold and crew closley
examined. english fleet off falmouth. 3 pressd men
brought abd. and put along with us.

29th. this morning Got under way in falmouth harbour the wind at S W fresh Breeze, the English fleet off
the Deadman. at 4 in the afternoon came to anchor
plymouth A brest the stone house in a small Bite within
80 yds. of the shore. the tide coming in heare runs verry
strong Theare is one flag flying at the fore top glt. mt.

hd. on the hill to the westd. of the sound of plymouth is a camp about 1000 Men at 5 in the afternoon Brought too Mill prison. The officer Lieut. haris have behaved verry politley. brought me a by road, not insulted by any mob. Confined to a room over the Guard house wh. 2 centrys.

30th. this day nothing verry particular to me. at night moved too the Black hole in the french yard where theare was some french dezarters. A horrid room. . . .

31. this morning took out of the Black hole brought to the room I was first put in. Several people heare say I am that Conyngham who Broke out of fortune prison. A soldier, the name of Davis, who came particularly to see me Declared before me he well knew that Conyngham that I was not that person. Others heare will heave that I am from Devonshire. I understand the Order of putting me in the Black hole was from the Capt of the Guarde his name, under schackles Nothing very remarkabble. I find the Serjeant of the Guard more strick—I not permitt the centrys to speak. at night put into the Black hole. recd. a Letter from Wm. heysham prisoner of War.

1st. August in the morning took out of the Black hole. I have been told the reason of this usage that I cannot be admitted into the prison where the AM. is without being taken before a Justice & Committed by him. Sundays, thursdays and fridays, the post comes in and Goes out of plymouth the Capt. of the Brig tapley called. his behaviour not like a Generous enemy, A middle size man, pocks Marks. came with him, md. use of some words very disrespective & some others of same company, &c. &c. I find very strick Orders Given the

Centinel every hour or two. A Gentleman Capt. of Militia, Mr. parsons. insisted that I was that Conyngham who broke out of fortune prison and took adam and three others with me   thiss was in May 78, Lodgd. in the Black Hole as usall.

2d. August in the Morning took out of the Black. hole. I find Capt. taylor of the Guarde a reasonable man well Disposed. Conversed with me and more moderate than I am used to of Late At night put into the Black hole As Customary.

3d. August. in the morning took out of the Black hole. brought to the room I. was first put in. A ensigne of the Devonshire Militia the Name Schiver from Gosport positively he says he knows me well. At night lodge as usall in the Black hole. I have been I have been told that Mr. Arnold is Committd. to Mill prison The english fleet I understand keeps nigh thiss coast. I have been told that Corporal Spelman being on Dutty at fortune prison under the command of Capt. parsons of the Middle Sex Militia, that an America prisoneer the Name of White said Corporal shot him with a ball through the Boddy.

4th. in the morning took out of the Black hole as usall, Dark weather & cool. At night put in the Black hole as usall Capt. Wise of the Guarde of the Devonshire Militia verry strickt, he cautioned not to Convey my Ideas by books to the Am prisoneers, if he found I did, should be Deterd. the privilege of Reading—

5th. took out of the Black hole as usall. Capt. Whitpew of the Guarde verry politley let me have the Liberty of the rooms. thiss Gentlm. treatted me verry politley. this is the Greatest Liberty I have been showne since I have been heare. Not put into the Black. hole. Sleep in the room. I have Liberty by day.—

6th. I find a verry material Difference in the officers orders of the Guarde. At 7 in the evening Lodged in the Black hole at 8 in the morning took out.—

7th. August. took before the Justices of the peace, after many questions, Commt. to mill prison for high treason thiss prision the have a Good Yard. the prisoneers have such a time to walk in the air Nothing but what is customary in such places to the 17th. A fleet of plymouth we are told is the french and english all day a canonading from Mill prison could perceive the smoak. A Great number of people collected to the forts in the night firing the Alarm Guns the inhabitants busy throwing up Lines Ditches &c. All in confusion—

20th. we find the fleet that appeared on the 17th. & 18th. to be the french fleet on the 18th. at night & 19 fresh Gale from the eastward that it is to be supposed has drove the french fleet to the Westd. the english fleet out we have no Account off. no news worthey of observation, but in the Old Stile, Double Guardes round our prison and at every corner. thiss day Capt.   of the Guarde came into the different apartments and verry politely enquired into the manner we wheare treatted. he said while he comd. he would inspect to the provisions to see if it was to contracts.

20th. one of the Am prisoners having some words with the Centinall, verry narrowley escaped the plunge of his bayonett Capt. parsons of the Guarde came into the prison yard behaved verry improper—

21st. nothing very material Capt. kelly of the Guarde verry polite we are told the Ardent is taken by the french. 22d. thiss day a ensigne the Name of Banton, of the Guarde behaved and used abusive Language.

23d. the french prisoneers marchd. from Mill prison, fife & drum.

24th. Capt. Burt of the Willtshire Militia came into the yard Made use of threatning expressions such as shooting and spitting the prisoners.

from the 24th to 29th nothing worthey of notice provisions verry ordinary for some time past this day a man called at the prison Gate he declared he was my brother could not persuade him to the contrary. Tin miners employd. throryhing ditches round plymouth & Dock.

31st. nothing verry material this day the prisoners having a dispute with the Baker A scuffle insued. the Guarde orderd into the prison yd. prisoners orderd in after some little dispute. the prisoners having nothing to eat for 14 hours Opned the door came into the yd. the Guarde Orderd to Load & prime after some Conversation with the officer of the Guarde the doors opend.

1 Sept. A fleet in sight Sr. Charles hardy put back to St. helena

7th. A Captain Martin calld at the Gate after some little conversation he says knows C. Conyngham well formeley belonging to Guersnsey.

28th Sept. A Capt. Dunn called to see me. . . . A bout the 10th. Octobr. a Singalure circumstance. A soldier who had stole a pair of Buckles had pawnd them was detectted he declared that C. Cony. had Gave them to him to pawn for him.

28th Octobr. provisions verry bad & little of it.

30th. A Mr. Cummings called at the prison gate— ofered me his services.

Notice in The Remembrancer[1]

Captain Conyngham was brought from New York to Falmouth, on board the Sandwich Packet, was kept in irons the whole voyage and sent ironed to Pendennis Castle, from which he was in a few weeks removed to Mill Prison, Plymouth, on petition to the Board of Sick and Hurt, and is now rated as an exchangeable prisoner, together with near 190 of his countrymen, for whom there is a cartel settled, and now passing to and from France.

[THE MARINE COMMITTEE TO JOHN BEATTY[2][3]]

June 2d, 1779

Sir

We have been informed that Captain Gustavus Conyngham late Commander of the Cutter Revenge which sailed from this Port, now a Prisoner at New York is ill treated under pretence that he had acted without a Commission when early in the year 1777 he commanded a small armed vessel called the Surprize and in her captured the Harwich Packet in the British Channel.

The Enclosed Certificates, from Silas Deane Esqr and two other Gentlemen then in France under whose direction that vessel was fitted out and who are well

[1] London, 1779, p. 341.
[2] A colonel of the Continental army, and Commissary-General of Prisoners.
[3] Marine Committee Letter-book, pp. 217–218.

acquainted with the whole transaction fully satisfy us that Captain Conyngham did not act without authority but that he was duly commissionated to command that vessel. Of this you will please to acquaint the British Commissary, and we request you will inform yourself in what manner Captain Conyngham is treated, which if you discover to be rigorously or with undue severity, it is our desire that you inform the Commissary that retaliation will be made unless they change their conduct towards him. We are Sir

Your Hble Servants

[THE MARINE COMMITTEE TO JOHN BEATTY[1]]

Colonel John Beatty
   Sir   July 5th 1779

We wrote you the 2d. Ultimo respecting Captain Gustavus Conyngham of the Revenge Cutter the receipt of which you have not yet acknowledged. We want to know if you have received that Letter and what you have done in consequence of it. We have been told that Captain Conyngham has lately been sent off from New York for England the truth of which we desire to know and request you will inform us. We have seen your letter of the 20th June respecting Mr Nicholas Ogden. it is our desire that you offer him in Exchange for Mr. James Willing now a Prisoner at New York. We request you will write to us shortly respecting Captain Conyngham. We are sir

Your hble servants

[1] Marine Committee Letter-book, p. 225.

Petition of a Number of Inhabitants of Philadelphia[1]

Honorable Sirs   Philadelphia July 14th 1779

Affected at the distressed situation of a fellow Citizen, and feeling it our duty as well as our disposition to render him every service in our power, we humbly entreat the attention of this Honorable House to the case of Captain Gustavus Conyngham now a Prisoner with the enemy, closely confined and ordered by them to be sent to England. We have learned his condition from his own Letter to his distressed wife dated on board the Packet Boat June 12th 1779 a Copy of which we beg leave to lay before you.

"Sorry I am to inform you that I am on board and to be sent to England. I have in part lost my health and cannot live long in this manner. If it pleases God to call me to himself out of this troublesome World, I live in hopes to meet you in Paradise. I am not able to write more. If possible rest contented. I would leave this western world easy if I had you with me. I must once more I believe for the last time recommend you to God, and live as contented as possible. Your loving affectionate husband 'till Death

"GUSTAVUS CONYNGHAM."

[1] Papers of the Continental Congress, No. 42, VI, folio 218.

Our Prayer to this Honorable House is that you would be pleased to claim Captain Gustavus Conyngham as a Citizen of the United States and demand the reason why he is thus distinguished by a severity of treatment; and if such satisfaction and relief as the case may require be not instantly given, that you will take measures for the security of his Person by holding some Prisoner or Prisoners of the enemy, of the same Rank or similar thereto, subject to the same pains and punishment as they may inflict on him.   And we are the more urgent in this request as many of us (being Masters of Vessels) may probably fall into the hands of the enemy, and are apprehensive if a just line of retaliation is not agreed upon, of suffering the same harsh and ignominious treatment.

And your Petitioners will ever Pray.

Andw. Hodge
John Nixon
Saml Meridith
Wm. Davis
Jno. Patton
Saml. Crawford
John Barclay
Saml. C Morris
Davd. Duncan
Jno. Shee
James Caldwell
Wm. Bradford
John Mease
Seth Harding
James Montgomery

Thos Barclay
Robt Morris
John Donnaldson
Saml. Caldwell
Mathw. Irwin
Thos. Pryor
A. Stewart
Wm. Turnbull
Robt Totten
Thomas Irwin
James Ash
Alexr. Foster
Sharp Delany
Cad. Morris
Geo Meade

Jas. Craig junr.
Andw Caldwell
John Wilson
John McNachtane
Tho. Bell
Harmon Courten
Thomas Housten
Saml. Howell Jun
William Budden
Jay Castle
Thos. Read
William Brown
W. Gamble
Thos Moore
Stephen Beasly
Isaac Roach
Nathan Bogs
John Rice
Edw Yorke
Ephraim Doane
J. M. Nesbitt
David H Conyngham
Alexr. Nesbitt
Rich. Bache
James Mease

Francis Lewis Junr
Joseph Bullock
Blair McLenachan
John Pringle
J. Wilkinson
Thos. Smith
Robert Gray
Thomas Morris
Wm. Hall
Benjamin G. Eyre
Jas. Budden
J. Metcher
Isaac Wikoff
Thos Fitzsimons
Robt. Bridges
William Sharp
Frans. Gurney
Benjn. Davis
John Benezet
Wm. Lawrence
Isaac Cox
James Wilson
Andw. Hodge Junr.
Hugh Hodge

Endorsed: Petition of a number of inhabitants of Philada relative to Capt Conyngham Read 17 July 1779 Referred to Mr Morris Mr Dickinson Mr Whipple

[ANN CONYNGHAM TO THE PRESIDENT OF CONGRESS[1]]

Hond Sir   Philada. July 17, 1779

I beg leave to trouble your Excellency, and the Honorable Congress with the perusal of the inclos'd Letter from my Husband Capt Gustavus Conyngham late Commander of the Cutter Revenge now a Prisoner & in Irons on board A British Packet bound to England.

As these Extraordinary and (in the present Stage of the War between Britain & America) Singular Cruelties exercised upon the Person of my Husband have been inflicted in consequence of his Zeal and successfull exertions against the common Enemy in the English Channell where he first hoisted the American Flag, I take the Liberty of calling the Attention of Congress to his distressed situation and of requesting that they would be pleased to take such steps for his relief as have in similar Instances prevented the Execution of the bloody and Vindictive purposes of the Enemy upon the Officers & Citizens of these States. I hope it is unnecessary to say any thing to the Honble Congress of my Distress upon this Occasion. To have lost a worthy & belov'd Husband in Battle fighting for the honour & Liberties of his Country would have been a light affliction. But to hear of a Person thus connected being chained to the Hold of a Ship, in vain looking back towards the belov'd Country for which he had fought, wasting his health and spirits in hopeless Grief, and at

---

[1] The letter is in the Papers of the Continental Congress, No. 78, V, folio 371.

last compleating the measure of his sufferings by an ignominious Death under —— Good God my heart shudders! at the thought. Forbid it Heaven, Forbid it Honble Gentlemen the Guardians of the Lives and Happiness of the good People of these States that a Freeman & a Soldier of America, should even fear or feel a moments distress or pain from the hand of Eng-lishmen, Unrevenged.

The Delay of a single Hour may fix my Husband's fate for ever, Pardon me therefore whilst I once more intreat your immediate Attention to his Case; consider Sir's the safety of your numerous officers, and soldiers, by Sea and Land is connected with that of my Husband. This I presume will be a sufficient motive with you to procure Justice for him & to afford some Consolation to,

Honble. Sir's & Gentlemen,

Your most obedient

and most devoted

ANN CONYNGHAM.

Extract from the Journals of Congress, July 17, 1779[1]

A letter, of 17th, from Ann Conyngham, and a peti-tion from a number of the inhabitants of Philadelphia, were read, representing that Gustavus Conyngham,

---

[1] Journals of the Continental Congress, Vol. XIV, p. 844. The letter of Ann Conyngham is in the Papers of the Continental Congress, No. 78, V, folio 371 ; the Pennsylvania petition, dated the 14th, is in No. 42, VI, folio 218.

now a prisoner with the enemy, is closely confined and ordered to be sent to England, and praying that measures may be taken for the security of his person:

Ordered, that the same be referred to a committee of three:

The members chosen, Mr. [Gouverneur] Morris, Mr. [John] Dickinson, and Mr. [William] Whipple.

Extract from the Journals of Congress, July 17, 1779[1]

The committee to whom were referred the petition and letter respecting Gustavus Conyngham, brought in a report; Whereupon

Resolved, That the following letter from the secretary of Congress be written to the admiral or other commanding officer of the fleets or Ships of his Britannic Majesty, lying in the harbor of New York:

"Sir: I am directed by the Congress of the United States of America to inform you that they have received evidence that Gustavus Conyngham a citizen of America, late commander of an armed vessel in the Service of the said states, and taken on board a private armed cutter, hath been treated in a manner contrary to the dictates of humanity and the practice of Christian civilized nations. I am ordered in the name of Congress to demand that good and sufficient reasons be given for this conduct, or that the said Gustavus Con-

---

[1] Journals of the Continental Congress, Vol. XIV, p. 849.

yngham be immediately released from his present rigorous and ignominious confinement.

"With all due respect, I have the honor to be,

"Sir, your most obedient and humble servant."

Resolved, That unless a satisfactory answer be received to the foregoing letter on or before the first day of August next, the Marine Committee do immediately cause to be confined in close and safe custody such, and so many persons as they may think proper in order to abide the fate of the said Gustavus Conyngham.

Ordered, That the above letter be immediately transmitted to New York by the Board of War, and that copies of the said letter and resolution be delivered to the wife of Captain Conyngham and to the petitioners.

[SIR GEORGE COLLIER TO THE SECRETARY OF CONGRESS[1]]

Sir   Raisonable, off New-York, 24th July, 1779.

I have the honour to inform you by direction of Sir George Collier, Commodore and Commander in Chief of his Majesty's ships in America, that he has received the letter you wrote him by order of the Congress, respecting Gustavus Conyngham; and I have it in command from the Commodore to say, that, not holding himself accountable for his conduct to any of his Majesty's subjects in this country, he is still less inclined to answer demands when they are made in the uncivil

[1] This letter is in the Papers of the Continental Congress, No. 78, XV, folio 477. Printed in the Pennsylvania Gazette, August 4, 1779 (from Rivington's New-York Royal Gazette, New-York, July 28).

way they appear to him in your letter of the 17th instant. He however is pleased to bid me inform you, that no prisoners are ever treated (to his knowledge) by the King's Officers contrary to the dictates of humanity; and as it is the practice of civilized nations to punish criminals in the usual course of justice, Gustavus Conyngham, whom you enquire after, stands in this predicament, and is therefore sent to England to receive that punishment from his injured country, which his crimes shall be found to deserve.

I am, Sir,
  Your very humble servant,
   JOHN MARR,
    Secretary to the Commander in Chief
Charles Thomson, Esq.

[BENJAMIN FRANKLIN TO MR. DIGGES[1] [2]]

Dear Sir,—   Passy, Augt 20, 1779.

I hear Capt. Cunningham is confined in England a prisoner. I desire you would take care to supply him with necessaries, that a brave man may not suffer for want of assistance in his distress. I ordered payment of your bill, but it has not yet appeared.

    I am ever
     Your affectionate B. F.

[1] An American merchant in London, who, a few years later, turned out to be a British spy, a defaulter, and an embezzler of nearly all the money he had received for the use of the prisoners.
[2] In Hale's Franklin in France, Vol. I, p. 344.

List of American Prisoners committed to Old Mill Prison, England, during the War[1]

(Extract)

Cutter taken, only Captain committed Aug 23, 1779.
—Gustavus Cunningham, Philadelphia, ran away.

[THE MARINE COMMITTEE TO JOHN BEATTY[2]]

Col. John Beatty
   Sir
                             August 31. 1779

As we understand that Captain Porterfield of the Ship Jason is in close confinement at Boston on Account of the enemys treatment of Captain Gustavus Conyngham, and as we have chosen Lieutenant Hele[3] of the British Navy as a fitter person for that purpose and have him now confined at this place, we desire that you will give Orders that Captain Porterfield be treated in the same manner with the other Prisoners of War provided his present rigourous treatment has been ordered in retaliation for Capt. Conyngham.

We are Sir

Your Hble Servant

---

[1] In the New England Historical and Genealogical Register, Vol. XIX (1865), p. 138.

[2] Marine Committee Letter-book, p. 230.

[3] Christopher Hele, Lieutenant, R. N.

[JONATHAN NESBIT TO BENJAMIN FRANKLIN[1]]

Sir,—   L'Orient, Sept. 22d, 1779.

By the Brig Retaliation, Capt. Kolloch, which left Philadelphia the 10th August, I have received letters informing me that Capt. G. Conyngham, late commander of the Cutter Revenge, had the misfortune to be taken last spring by the Galatea and sent into New York, from whence he has been sent to England with a design to have him tryed for Piracy. They pretend to say that he took the Harwich Packet without having any commission, which your excellency must know to be false,—as I believe you were in Paris at the time that his Commission and orders were delivered him. The Commission under which he acted as Captn of the Revenge is dated, I apprehend, after the taking of the Harwich packet.[2] It is on this circumstance, no doubt, that the charge of piracy is founded. His first commission was taken from him in Dunkirk after he was put in gaol, and sent up to Paris, and I think was lodged in the hands of Monsr le Comte de Vergennes. I have to request that your Excellency will do everything in your power to prevent this poor fellow from suffering. Considering the smallness of his vessel and the difficulty he labored under when he first left France, he has done a great deal for the service of his country. He has done

[1] In Hale's Franklin in France, Vol. I, pp. 344–5.
[2] Nesbit is here wrong. The first commission was dated March 1, 1777; the second, May 2 of the same year. The Harwich packet was taken on May 7.

so much harm to the enemy that he can expect no mercy at their hands, and if they can find any pretence whatever, they will certainly destroy him. Capt. Kolloch informs me that he was sent home in irons. I should certainly have heard from him was he not already confined. I once more take the liberty to recommend the unhappy man's case to your excellency's particular attention.

I have the honor to be wth great respect,

JONATHAN NESBIT.

[BENJAMIN FRANKLIN TO JONATHAN NESBIT[1]]

Sir,—   Passy, September 29, 1779.

Captain Conyngham has not been neglected. As soon as I heard of his arrival in England, I wrote to a friend[2] to furnish him with what money he might want, and to assure him that he had never acted without a commission. I have been made to understand in answer that there is no intention to prosecute him, and that he was accordingly removed from Pendennis Castle and put among the common prisoners at Plymouth, to take his turn for exchange. The Congress, hearing of the threats to sacrifice him, put three officers in close confinement to abide his fate, and acquainted Sir George Collier with their determination, who probably wrote to the

[1] MSS. Department of State; printed in Wharton's Revolutionary Diplomatic Correspondence, Vol. III, p. 350.
[2] Mr. Digges. See p. 183.

British Ministers. I thank you for informing me what became of his first commission. I suppose I can now easily recover it, to produce on occasion. Probably the date of that taken with him, being posterior to his capture of the pacquet, made the enemy think that they had an advantage against him. But when the English government have encouraged our sailors intrusted with our vessels to betray that trust, run away with the vessels, and bring them into English ports, giving such traitors the value as if good and lawful prizes, it was foolish imprudence in the English commodore to talk of hanging one of our captains for taking a prize without commission.

I have the honour to be, with great esteem, sir,

B. FRANKLIN.

[BENJAMIN FRANKLIN TO M. DE SARTINE[1]]

Passy, October 19, 1779.

I received the letter your excellency did me the honor of writing to me the 14th instant relating to the claim of Francois Vermeille to be paid wages and prize money due to him from Captain Cunningham, commander of the Revenge privateer. I find on inquiry that the said Vermeille and several other French sailors who said

[1] MSS. Department of State; printed in Wharton's Diplomatic Correspondence of the American Revolution, Vol. III, pp. 386–387.

they had belonged to that vessel, having been a long time imprisoned in England, were exchanged by the last cartel.

When they passed through this place on their return to Dunkirk I gave them some money to help them on their journey, and advised them to apply to Mr. Coffin, our present agent there, who I supposed could inform them who it was that did the business of equipping Captain Cunningham, and must therefore know what men were shipped, on what terms, what they had received in advance, and what prizes were taken (of all which I was totally ignorant), and by that means ascertain their claims, in which I desired Mr. Coffin to assist them, so that I might take the proper means of obtaining for them what is their due. Mr. Coffin wrote me a letter in answer to my request, of which I enclose a copy. Mr. Deane and Mr. Hodge, who were concerned in that enterprise, are neither of them at present in France, but Mr. Deane is soon expected here. Captain Conyngham is now a prisoner in England, but I hope will soon be exchanged and appear here. Nothing is more just than that these men should be paid what is really due to them; but as I had no concern in the affair and never saw any account of the prizes taken and know nothing of the agreement made with the sailors, it is impossible for me to adjust their claims. All I can do is to communicate them to the proper persons and solicit, which I shall do warmly, that justice be done.

With great respect, etc.

[BENJAMIN FRANKLIN TO M. LE BRUN[1]]

Sir: Passy, October 25, 1779.

Mr. Arthur Lee has not been recalled, the States in Congress being equally divided on the question; but he has mentioned to me his intention of returning immediately to America, as no certain provision has been made for his support in Spain.

Captain Conyngham was sent to England in irons, to be tried for his life as a pirate. The Congress ordered some English prisoners of equal rank to be put in irons, by way of reprisal, to abide his fate. Since his arrival in England his irons have been taken off and he is treated as the other prisoners, and will probably soon be exchanged. Here are a number of Frenchmen that had served with him, and being put on board one of his prizes afterwards carried into England, were kept prisoners there till lately, when he exchanged them. They demand their wages and a share of his prizes. I shall be obliged to Messrs. de Lagraner for any information they may be pleased to send me. What has been done with the produce of these prizes sold in Spain?

With great respect, etc.

[1] MSS. Department of State; printed in Wharton's Diplomatic Correspondence of the American Revolution, Vol. III, pp. 393–394.

[GUSTAVUS CONYNGHAM TO BENJAMIN FRANKLIN[1]]

Dr Sir,—   Amsterdam, Nov. 18th, 1779.

I have the pleasure to inform you that on the 3d instant, with about 50 of our unfortunate countrymen, broke out of Mill prison. I brought 3 officers with me. I came by the way of London, it being the safest. At London we meet with our good friend Mr. Digges, who did everything in his power to serve me and all his countrymen that chance to fall in his way. Happy we to have such a man among that set of tyrants they have in that country. The treatment I have received is unparalleled. Irons, dungeons, hunger, the hangmans cart I have experienced. I shall set off from here the 19th for Dunkirk. There I shall be glad to hear from you. I shall always be ready to serve my country, and happy should I be to be able to come alongside some of those petty tyrants. I find something of the effects of my confinement. In a short time wil be able to retaliate. I should at this time go out with Capt. Jones or in the squadron, could I have heard from you. I should be glad to go for the Continent if a good opportunity served. In this I shall take your advice, and act accordingly. The cash Mr. Digges supplied me with, and some necessaries I got at Plymouth the amt could not procure; the friend we have at Plymouth is obliged to act with the greatest caution. Mr. Redmond Conyngham, in Ireland, has ordered me some little supply through the hands of David Hartley of London, a mortel enemy of America by all accounts. From your most obet. and very humble servt.,   G. CONYNGHAM.

[1] In Hale's Franklin in France, Vol. I, pp. 346–7.

[BENJAMIN FRANKLIN TO GUSTAVUS CONYNGHAM[1]]

Sir,— Passy, Nov. 22, 1779.

It gave me great pleasure to hear of your escape out of prison, which I first learnt from 6 of the men who broke out with you and came to France in a boat. I was then anxious lest you should be retaken, and I am very glad indeed to hear of your safe arrival at Amsterdam. I think it will be best for you to stay awhile at Dunkirk, till we see what becomes of the little squadron from Holland, for which it is said the English are lying in wait with a superior force. The Congress resented exceedingly the inhuman treatment you met with, and it ordered three English officers to be confined in the same manner, to abide your fate.

There are some Frenchmen returned to Dunkirk who were put by you into one of your first prizes, which was afterwards carried into England. I wish you would adjust their claims of wages, prize money, &c., and put them in a way of getting what may be due to them.

I write to Mr. Coffyn by this post, to supply you with necessaries. You will be as frugal as possible, money being scarce with me, and the calls upon me abundant.

With great esteem, I have, &c.

[1] In Hale's Franklin in France, Vol. I, pp. 347–8.

[JOHN PAUL JONES TO BENJAMIN FRANKLIN[1]]

(Extract)   Alliance, Texel, Novr. 29th. 1779

I wrote from Amsterdam the 11th. Octr. a letter to you which I fear has miscarried. I have the pleasure to inform you that Capt. Cunningham is now here with me.

Extract from the Journals of Congress, December 13, 1779[2]

A memorial of Christopher Hele, was read, praying to be exchanged, and to have leave to go to New York upon his parole for a few days, to procure a person in his room:[3]

Resolved, That Mr. Hele be informed that the prayer of his memorial cannot be granted until Captain Cunningham is released, as it has been determined that he must abide the fate of that officer.

[1] In the Franklin Papers (Library of Congress), 193–247.
[2] Journals of the Continental Congress, Vol. XV, p. 1373.
[3] This memorial, dated December 10, is in the Papers of the Continental Congress, No. 41, IV, folio 99.

[GUSTAVUS CONYNGHAM TO BENJAMIN FRANKLIN[1]]

Texel Road, December 22, 1779.

Honourable Sir,—

I wrote you last from Amsterdam. At that time informed of my going to Dunkirk; but meeting with Comd. Jones prevented me, and supposing the Alliance will be ordered home as soon as she may get to France. The hurry I was obliged to leave England could not get my account with me. Mr. Digges was to send it to Dunkirk as soon as he could get it from Plymouth. I hope ere this you have a settlement from the Geoine of the prizes left in care of Mr. Lagoanese & Co. Should be glad to know the result in that quarter. The two west india men that was given up by the Court of France, they paying the captors. I must think we have an undoubted right to be paid for the packet and Brig. of ——. The Brig had a valuable cargo. In reality they should [pay] for the confinement we were under. I shall acquaint you of the many favours I received since I became a captive. 1st, in New York, that Sir George Collier ordered irons on my legs, with a centry on board the ship. Mr. Collier going on an expedition ordered me to jaole, there put me into the condemned room. The first night a cold plank my bed, a stone for a pillow. 2nd night allowed a something to lay on; in this horrid room was kept for eight days without the least morsel of bread, or anything but water, from the keeper of the

[1] In the Complete Works of Benjamin Franklin (ed. Bigelow, 1888), Vol. VI, p. 482.

prison. After many notes, &c., sent to the jailer, at last he made his appearance. After expostulating of the impropriety of such treatment he told me *he had such orders,* but would take it upon himself to release me on my giving him my strongest assurances I would not make my escape. I readily consented,—it not being in the power of man to get out of the condemned room. By all accounts this the first instance of this jailers humanity. A creature after Clinton's own heart. In the prison of New York I continued till that tyrant Collier returned. A stranger to his mode of war would be certain he was from Gambia, or that quarter. Then I was told to get ready to go on board the prison-ship, was moved to a separate apartment in the prison; then a pair of criminal irons put on my legs, weight 50 pounds; at the door, put into the hangman's cart,—all in form as if bound to the gallows. I was put then into a boat and took alongside of the Raisonable then showed a paper, signed Commd. Jones, ordering me to be sent to England in the packet. In those Irons I was brought to Pendennis Castle. Then not contented, they manacled my hands with a new fashioned pair of ruffels fitted very tite. In this condition I was kept there 15 or 16 days, then brought to Plymouth and lodged in the black hole for eight days, before they would do me the honour of committing me on suspicion of high treason on his majesties high seas; then put into Mill prison, where we committed treason through his earth and made our escape. This, Sir, is an account of their favors, insults excepted. I must acquaint your excellency that the poor unfortunate prisoners in Plymouth are in a most distressed situation. The donation, when I left that, had been at 6d per week. I am afraid could they not be

exchanged soon, will be obliged to enter in their service. They cannot live on the Government allowance. I hope to have the favour of a letter from you. I am, sir,
Your most obedient servant,

G. CONYNGHAM.

[JOHN ADAMS TO THE PRESIDENT OF CONGRESS[1]]

Sir: Paris, February 17, 1780.

It is necessary that I should inform Congress in what manner I have been able to procure money to defray my expenses in my long journey through the greatest part of Spain and France to this city.

On my arrival at Ferrol I was offered the loan of money by the French consul, M. de Tournelle, who at the same time told me there was a gentleman at Corunna, M. Michael Lagoanere, who had heretofore acted as an American agent at that place, and who would be very happy to supply me. On my arrival at Corunna, M. Lagoanere did me the honor of a visit, and offered me every assistance in cash, otherwise telling me at the same time he had some money in his hands which he supposed belonged to the United States, being part of the proceeds of some prizes heretofore made by Captain Cunningham. That this money, however, had been attached in his hands by some Spanish merchant, who had commenced a lawsuit against

[1] MSS. Department of State; printed in Wharton's Diplomatic Correspondence of the American Revolution, Vol. III, p. 499.

Captain Cunningham. I accordingly received three thousand dollars for myself and Mr. Dana, and a letter of credit on the house of Cabarous, at Bayonne, for as much more as I should have occasion for. On our arrival at Bayonne Mr. Dana and I received of that house fifty louis d'ors, and a bill of exchange on another house of the same name and family at Bordeaux for the like sum, our expenses having exceeded all our computations at Corunna, as our journey was necessarily much longer than we expected, on account of the uncommon bad weather and bad roads. This bill was paid upon sight. So that, upon the whole, we have received the amount of seventeen thousand four hundred livres, all on account of M. Lagoanere, of Corunna. Of this sum Mr. Dana has received the amount of four thousand nine hundred and seventy-one livres and fifteen sols, and I have received twelve thousand four hundred and twenty-eight livres and five sols, for which sums we desire to be respectively charged in the treasury books of Congress.

As this money is expended, if M. Lagoanere should draw upon us for it, all the authority we have to draw upon his excellency the minister here will not enable us to pay it; and if M. Lagoanere should be so happy as to avoid the attachment and leave us to account with Congress for this money, the small sum we are empowered to receive from his excellency will go a very little way in discharging our expenses. We must, therefore, pray that Congress would forward us authority to draw upon his excellency for the amount of our salaries annually, which, without all doubt, will be paid.

I have the honor to be, with the highest respect, etc.,

JOHN ADAMS.

[GEORGE HOOPER TO GUSTAVUS CONYNGHAM[1]]

Capt Gustavus Conyngham   London 13 July 1780.

Sir

By letter from Messrs. Holdsworth and Co. of Dartmouth acquainting me of your being carried to Plimouth, I now Inclose you a letter from Mr. Thos. Hockley of Philadelphia under cover of one to me dated Augt. 7th. 1779 Desiring me to give you Creditt . . . as this will be Handed you by my Friend Joseph Squires Esqr. I have Desired him to take your bill on me for £20 or 30 should your Necessitys Require more a future Draft shall be duly Honoured, in your bills please to say to be placed to Acct. of Mr. Thos. Hockley, of Philadelphia, I hope soon we may meet as Friends, att present I can only wish you a speedy recovery of your Health and am

Sir

Your most Humble

St.   GEO HOOPER

(Addressed to Capt Gustavus Conyngham, att Plymouth. pr favor of Joseph Squires Esqr.)

[1] MSS. in the collection of Mr. James Barnes.

[JONATHAN NESBITT TO GUSTAVUS CONYNGHAM[1]]

Dear Sir   l'Orient July 26th: 1780

Your Letter of the 10th: Inst: which I receiv'd by the way of Morlaix, gave me great pleasure altho' dated from a Prison, for now your friends know where you are it is in their power to render you some assistance. you cannot conceive how unhappy we were to hear of your being taken; the more so as we understood you had fallen into the hands of a man who treated you with great inhumanity, and Doctor Brooke wrote his friends here that you were in a very poor state of health. I wrote last Post to Doctor Franklin, & represented to him your situation, and doubt not but he will use his utmost endeavors to get you exchanged as soon as possible, and like [letter is here torn] ith money or a Credit to En [torn away] and purchase such things as may [torn away] your health.—but for fear that the multiplicity of business may prevent him from remitting you immediately, I have wrote this day to my Banker in Paris to order his Correspondent in London to honor your drafts to the amount of Fifty pounds sterling, and at same time to desire his said Correspondent to write you immediately to acquaint you thereof. but at same time if Mr. Franklin gives you a sufficient Credit, or furnishes you with money, I must request that you will not make use of mine.

It will give me great pleasure to hear that you are

[1] MSS. in the collection of Mr. James Barnes.

Exchanged, & to see you here shortly where you will have constant opportunitys of returning home. I have lately receiv'd Letters from my Brother who seems very anxious for your return [torn away] a fine Ship [torn away]

I must desire above all things that you will endeavor to regain your health for which purpose it is Necessary that you should keep up your Spirits. Consider how many men there are in your situation who have no friends in a Capacity to render them the smallest assistance, whereas you have many that are able & willing to render you every service. I remain with Sentiments of the most sincere friendship

> Dear Sir
> Your most hble Servt.
> JONATN. NESBITT.

[GEORGE HOOPER TO GUSTAVUS CONYNGHAM[1]]

> London 25 Augt. 1780

Capt. Gustavus Conyngham
Sir

I duly Rec'd. yours of the 7th Covering one for Mr. Thos. Hockley which I shall forward by the first good ship.

I have made Inquiery att ye. Sick & Wounded if any

---

[1] MSS. in the collection of Mr. James Barnes.

Exchange of prisoners is soon expectd. Rec'd for answer that nothing of the kind is expected yett.

I am Glad to hear you are Recovering your Health again, its what I wish you a long Continuance off and am Sir your obdt. Humble
St.
GEO. HOOPER

(Addressed to Capt Gustavus Conyngham, Mill Prison, Plymouth)

[JONATHAN NESBITT TO GUSTAVUS CONYNGHAM[1]]

Dear Conyngham   L'Orient Jany. 24th, 1781

I this day receiv'd your Letter of the 25th. Decr: which really gave me pleasure tho' dated in Prison, for I had heard of your escape & being retaken, & really feard that hard treatment had put an end to your existence & sufferings together—the Papers inclosed in your Letter are sent forward this day for Philadelphia, and I have caus'd Copys to be taken (fearing that the originals might miscarry) which shall be forwarded by other Vessels very shortly.— I hope Congress will take your situation into Consideration, & order one or more British officers to be treated in the same manner that you have been, untill satisfaction is made you; but cannot *flatter* you that they will do so, for the English officers that are Prisoners to the Americans are treated

---

[1] MSS. in the collection of Mr. James Barnes.

like Gentlemen (tho' few of them deserve the Caracter) whilst the Americans in the power of the English are treated like Dogs or worse than Dogs.—Almost the only instance of Retaliating was on advice being receiv'd of your treatment at New York & being sent to England in Irons, when the Congress thought proper to order a British officer then at Philadelphia on his Parole, into Prison, from which he was however releas'd in a very short time in Complaining of a slight indisposition.

The person in London employ'd to pay you the money which I order'd you, has constantly declared that he found it impossible, except thro' the hands of the Commissary, whom he had no orders to trust with it. I intend this day to give fresh orders, and at same time beg that you will endeavor to inform me if I can by any means convey money directly into your hands.—point out how it can be done & you may be assured of my attention thereto.

There are several very fine American Vessels now in this Port, all strongly Armed, by which I have Accounts from America as late as the 23d Decr. when every thing was favorable on our side—the American Privateers met with amazing success, not only the owners, but the officers & Seamen made fortunes,—I wish you were at liberty to take a turn amongst them & remain very sincerely

Dear Conyngham

Your most hble Servt:

JONATH: NESBITT.

P:S: I do not know how it happend that I did not inform you in my last Letters that your Negro boy Tom is Dead this long time.

[JONATHAN NESBITT TO GUSTAVUS CONYNGHAM[1]]

Dear Conyngham   L'Orient May 2d. 1781.

I have receiv'd your several favors of the 15 & 31st.
March & 10th, April, the last of which came to hand
this day. I cannot possibly answer particularly what
you say about the Negro boy Tom, but on Mr. Coffyn's
writing me that he was unwell & desiring to know what
should be done with him, I requested that he would
endeavor to get him cured & that I would be answerable
for the expences. Shortly after I heard of his Death,
and at same time an account of sd: Expences was transmitted me;— as for Fitzgerald, nothing could be expected from him, for the Boy was almost always sick,
and four years past I was told by Doctor that he could
not live long.—besides poor Fitzgerald, was, & still is
if living, Disorder'd in his sences in such a manner as
to be incapable of doing anything.

I have very little at present to say, being without any
News from America,—the English may bragg as much
as they will, but they have little to brag of in America,
where our brave Troops never meet them in equal Numbers, but what they defeat them, and from the last accots;
which come by the way of Spain, there is great Reason
to hope that the infamous Arnold & his Army will meet
the same fate as Burgoyne.

Mrs. Conyngham will write you this Post.—she has
determined to stay here untill she hears further from

[1] MSS. in the collection of Mr. James Barnes.

you, in which I think she is quite right, for certainly a Journey to England would be attended with many difficultys & disagreeable Circumstances, besides if an exchange was to take place, you might happen to be in this kingdom by the time she arrivd in England.—for my part I have heard no mention of an exchange of Prisoners. but wish most ardently that it may take place. —such a thing might be readily brought about if there were any English, Prisoners to the Americans, in this kingdom, but this is not the case, and I have already mention'd to you that there are no American Vessells cruizing in these Seas.

I have receiv'd powers of Attorney from Wm: Reed & Lambert Murphy to receive their part of Prize Money due for the prizes taken, by, & their services on board the Privateer called the Duc de Coigni, also their orders on Monsieur Re Moyoné.—you will please to inform them that I shall do everything possible to recover their Money, but untill I hear from Granvill, I cannot say how far I may succeed.

I remain, Dear Conyngham,

Your most hble. servt.

JONATN : NESBITT.

(Addressed to Captn. Gustavus Conyngham, Mill Prison, near Plymouth)

[BENJAMIN FRANKLIN TO COFFIN[1]]

Sir: Passy, March 23, 1781.

I received your favor of the 10th. I have heard nothing of Mr. Wharton since my former. The Ariel has not arrived, at least her arrival was not heard of at Boston the 11th of February, which makes me fear she has either been taken, or has been blown off the coast of North America by the N.W. winds of that country, and is gone perhaps to Martinique.

I am sorry you have had so much trouble with those people of Captain Cunningham. The affair has been very perplexing to me. The vessel was fitted out by Mr. Hodge. You certainly had no share in her or concern in fitting her out, and it was only at my request that you took the part of those people in advising them how to ascertain their dues. Mr. Hodge was apprehended here and put into the Bastile for arming her clandestinely in a French port, it being before the war between France and England. He is now in America; Captain Cunningham is in prison in England. When he was in Holland with Captain Jones I was in hopes he would have called at Dunkirk and then the affair might have been settled there, but he went directly to Spain, and in sailing from thence was taken. I sent to America the declaration of those men which you forwarded to me in 1779. I suppose it miscarried, for I never heard of its being received. I should be glad to serve them in obtaining their just demands, but those should be ascer-

---

[1] MSS. Department of State; printed in Wharton's Diplomatic Correspondence of the American Revolution, Vol. IV.

tained. They would do well, therefore, to renew their declaration upon oath, and make four copies of it, to be sent by different vessels to America. I will solicit that their claims be enquired into and an order obtained for the payment of what shall appear to be their just right. This can only be done in America, for nowhere else is there any account to be found of the produce of the prizes. With great esteem, etc.

[BENJAMIN FRANKLIN TO GUSTAVUS CONYNGHAM[1]]

Passy, June 20, 1781.

Sir:

I received with great pleasure the news of your being safely arrived at Dunkirk. Mrs. Conyngham is not yet come to Paris. I believe she has continued at L'Orient ever since her arrival. I shall write to her to-day to acquaint her with your escape.

Now you are at Dunkirk, I wish you would settle the demand of a number of men who went out with you from thence and were taken in a prize and carried into England. They have long worried me to be their advance money and wages and prize money, in which I could do nothing, having no information of what might be due to them. The minister here has applied to me in their behalf; and I know not what answer to make him till I hear from you. I am, etc.

[1] MSS. Department of State; printed in Wharton's Diplomatic Correspondence of the American Revolution, Vol. IV.

Memorial of Gustavus Conyngham to Congress[1]

To the Honorable the Delegates of the United States of North America in General Congress Assembled—

The Memorial of Gustavus Cunyngham Most Humbly Sheweth—

That your Memorialest on the first Day of March 1777 received from the Honorable Commissioners of the United States of North America at the Court of France a Commission of Congress appointing him a Captain in the Navy of the said States and to Command a Vessel then fitting out at Dunkirk on their Account, to Cruize against their Enemies, in which Vessel your Memorialist took the English Packet Boat going from Harwich to Holland, But there being no war at that time Between France and England and the Clandestine Equipment of an Armed Vessel in a French Port to Cruize against the English being therefore an Unjustifiable Proceeding, your Memorialist was apprehended by Order of the French Government and his papers seized among which was the said Commission, which was never restored to your Memorialist and Cannot now be found, all which facts are duly Certified by the Honble Benjamin Franklin Minister Plenepotentiary for the United States of America at the Court of France given at Passy the 7th day of August in the year of our Lord 1782 a true Copy of which Certificate / the origi-

[1] Papers of the Continental Congress, No. 41, II, folio 152.

nal remaining in the Hands, of Colo Walter Stewart of the Pennsylvania Line / is hereunto annexed, That your Memorialist is Desirous of being placed in the same Situation he was by virtue of the said Commission, He therefore prays Congress to take his Case into Consideration and either by a New Commission to be Granted him for that purpose or otherwise as to Congress shall seem best to reinstate him in his former Situation.

And Your Memorialist will ever pray &c

GUSTAVUS CONYNGHAM.

Certificate issued by Benjamin Franklin[1]

I do hereby Certify whom it may Concern that the Commissioners of the United States of America at the Court of France, Did issue on the first day of March One thousand seven hundred and seventy seven to Captain Gustavus Conyngham a Commission of Congress appointing him a Captain in the Navy of the said States and to Command a Vessel then fitting out at Dunkerque on their account to Cruise against their Enemies, in which Vessel he took the English packet Boat going from Harwich to Holland but there being no war at that time Between France & England, and the Clandestine Equipment of an Armed Vessel in a French port to Cruise against the English being therefore an unjus-

[1] Papers of the Continental Congress, No. 41, II, folio 154.

tifiable proceeding He was apprehended by Order of the French Government and his papers seized, among which was the said Commission, which was never restored and Cannot now be found. It is therefore that at the request of the said Capt. Conyngham, and to ascertain the Fact that such a Commission was issued to him, I give this Certificate at Passy this 7th day of August, 1782.

(Seal.)

B. FRANKLIN
Minister plenepotentiary from
the United States of America
at the Court of France.

Report of the Committee of the War[1]

[October 13, 1783]

The Committee of the War report

That the Memorial of Gustavus Conyngham be referred to the Agent of Marine and on the facts stated in the Memorial being made appear Resolved that he take order for carrying the prayer of the Memorialist into effect.

[1] Papers of the Continental Congress, No. 32, folio 523.

Report of Committee of Congress on Conyngham Memorial[1]

[January 5, 1784]

The Committee to whom was referred a Memorial from Gustavus Conyngham praying for the renewal of a Commission of Captain in the Navy of the U. S. receiv'd from the Commissioners in Paris in 1777 & lost by him, or to be re-instated in his former situation beg leave to report —— that such Commissions were intended for temporary expeditions only & not to give rank in the Navy; & therefore that the prayer of the said Memorialist cannot be granted.

[NESBITT & CO. TO GUSTAVUS CONYNGHAM[2]]

Philadelphia, Dec. 3, 1781.

Captn. G. Conyngham
    Dear Sir
        The foregoing is Copy of our last of St. James to which refer. DWC was yesterday favoured with yours

---

[1] Papers of the Continental Congress, No. 19, I, folio 621.
[2] MSS. in the collection of Mr. James Barnes.

18th Septn. to Captn. Josiah in respect to what you mention of coppering the new Ship we have wrote J N & Co. and directed them to act as you and them thought most for the Owners advantage, we again request you will not leave Europe untill all your affairs at Conrunna are fully settled and hope you will be able to lodge the money due there in J N & Co's hands otherwise neither you nor us will ever have any satisfaction made us, in respect to your affairs in our hands both before you went to Juland or what you lodged with us when last here the Ballances still remain with us unemployed the principal Reason for this was that we never thought the British would have sent you to England we daily expected your Release and as we were constantly building fine vessels we always supposed you would be glad to take the Command and an Interest in one of them besides as we never had any positive Order to employ your money we decided it most prudent to keep it ready for you. You'l observe we paid Mrs. C. several large sums and the Money due you by Patrick Moore never came to our Hands. Mr. Joseph Wilson claims fifteen Guineas as advanced you in England and which we mean to pay Him and Mr. Diggs writes his Brother he has a Demand on us for the same amount this with the Money advanced Mrs. C. on her going to France reduces your continental Ballance considerably & you'l observe that the Ballance due you by Mr. Enkine of Boston never has been settled nor any of it paid us that Gentn. was on board the Shililah & perished we pre-

sume with her his Partner Mr. Donnatona will soon administer to his Estate & we shall take Care of your Claim on so short Notice we have not been able to make you any Remittance by this Vessell but we shall take care to do it as soon as possible & before you are ready to leave France as to your Demands on the Brig Peggy both for the Bill you mention and other Moneys and for Her if J N has recovered any thing from her affairs its proper you should have that Amount settled & paid by Him & this we hope he is enabled to do long e'er this though we have not lately heard from him on the Subject we hope you will soon get the ship in the Water & that you will make up by your Success in Her for past Misfortunes, the Success of
Troops in capturing the British Army under D. Cornwallis will probably make some Alteration in Affairs in Europe if so tho your Ship may cost high She may still be a valuable Vessell as a Merchantman for peaceable Times & in such a Trade you would no Doubt have great Satisfaction though we think you are intituled to a little Revenge all Friends join in wishes for your safety I am with Compliments to Mrs. C.

Yr. humble Servants

I. M. NESBITT & CO.

ACCOUNT PRESENTED BY GUSTAVUS CONYNGHAM[1]

THE UNITED STATES OF AMERICA,
OWNERS OF THE LUGGER SURPRISE & CUTTER REVENGE

To GUSTAVUS CONYNGHAM, Dr.

	Martinique Cy	Reals Villon	Sterling	Penn. Currency
To Amount of my acct. rendered to the late Board of Treasury	.. ..	21,293 5	2381 ,,10	633 18
To do. Account omissions herewith	2892 ,,9,,	28,289 11	.. ..	48 ..
	£2892 ,,9,,	R49,582 ,,16	£2381 ,,10	£681 18

It is to be observed, that in the Settlement of this account, I am at least entitled to Interest at the rate of 6 p cent per Annum from the 25th day of March 1779 (when I exhibited my claim before the Navy Board) but in strict Equity an Interest ought to commence on the Prize Money at the time of the completion of the Sales, and on my Disbursements from the Date of the Advances.

G CONYNGHAM

Endorsed on back Coppy of Acct left in the Auditors Office Novr. 1t. 1791

[1] MSS. in the collection of Mr. James Barnes.

[ALEXANDER HAMILTON TO GUSTAVUS CONYNGHAM[1]]

Sir: Treasury Department July 5th 1793

I have to acknowledge the receipt of your note of the 1st instant, respecting your claim upon the United States, and to assure you that a report on the Petition, which was referred to me, will be made to Congress next session.
                          I am, Sir,
                               Your obedt. Servant,
Capt. Gustavus Conyngham.   A HAMILTON.

[*Endorsements by Conyngham*]

Capt. Conyngham once more takes the liberty of stating to the Secretary of the Treasury—that his old claim for services rendered to the United States during the last war—still remains undecided on, The Secretary of the Treasury having assured Capt. Conyngham by note dated July 5th 1793 that a report on his petition would be made to Congress at their next Session—he begs leave to urge to the Secretary his anxiety to have it one way or the other as speedily as possible determined—31st March 1794.

Philade. 28th May 1794

Capt. Conyngham feels himself under the necessity of stating—that from the assurances of the Secretary of

[1] MSS. in the collection of Mr. James Barnes.

[213]

the Treasury—he has anxiously waited for the Secy. report on his petition this Session of Congress—but as it has not yet been made—Cap. Conyngham once more earnestly requests the Secretary to report before the Close of the present Session—as it is a matter of importance to him to have it speedily decided.

Phila. Dec. 8th. 94

No report having yet been made on Cap. Conyngham's Petition to Congress—and the Sect. of the Treasury having *explicitly* assured the Cap. that it should be done during their last Session of Congress, He earnestly urges to the Secretary his great anxiety to have this tedious business determined if possible in the Course of the present Session—it being to the Cap. of serious importance.

Petition of Gustavus Conyngham to Congress[1]

Philadelphia Decr. 26 1797

To the Honourable the Senate & House of Representatives of the United States of America in Congress Assembled.

The petition of Gustavus Conyngham
Respectfully Sheweth

That he feels it incumbent on him once more to apply

[1]MSS. in the collection of Mr. James Barnes.

[214]

to your honourable Body, on a subject which has been of equal Anxiety and Importance to him, for many years past, without having been able to obtain any Decision on his Claim on the United States —— To recapitulate to your honourable Body his services and dangers during his command of the Revenge Cutter, or to paint in just and glowing Colours, the cruel & grevious Sufferings he experienced, during a long tedious captivity, would be at this time irrelative to the sole object of this petition, which is simply to request of your Honbl. Body, that his claim, of compensation for services rendered to his country, during her revolutionary War; should be decided on —— Altho' he has sent petition after petition, to the proper Authority from the year 1779, until his last petition to your Honble. Body in the year 1793, yet it remains to this day in the same state of Doubt & uncertainty to him, no investigation or report having yet been made.—

The nature of the Claim of your petitioner will be explicitly stated by him, to whom your Honourable Body, may think proper to refer it. That a speedy enquiry may be made, and an early decision adopted by your Honble. Body, is the Earnest & Solemn Prayer, of your Petitioner.—

GUSTAVUS CONYNGHAM.

Observations on the Report of Benjamin Walker Esq to the late Board of Treasury on the Subject of Capt. Gustavus Conyngham's claim against the United States, as commander of the Lugger Surprize & the Cutter Revenge.[1]

1st.. First. The Lugger Surprize was purchased, & fitted out by order of the Commissioners of the United States, and my commission given to me by Doctor Franklin in Paris; which commission, was sign'd by John Hancock, the then President of Congress, & dated in Philadelphia the 2nd. of May 1777; Attested by Charles Thompson Secy.—The revenge was also purchased, & fitted out by the same direction.

2nd. I know nothing of this, as I did not then, nor do I yet suppose it my duty to inquire into the costs and outfitts of the vessels I commanded.

3rd. The Lugger Surprize was never in my possession after I was cast into prison at Dunkirk—She remained there when I left that place in the Revenge Cutter.

4th. Several Prizes were made and put into the hands of Messrs. Legoneire & Co, how the Proceeds were disposed of I do not particularly know, but Messrs. Legoneire & Co. had the American Commissioners orders respecting them. See Copy of Arthur Lee

[1] MSS. in the collection of Mr. James Barnes.

Esq.'s Letter to Legoneire & Co. Dated Paris 21st. Nov. 1777.

5th. I received a Letter from Mr. Silas Dean to this purport, but I paid no regard thereto, as I afterwards received orders from the American Commissioners at Paris contradicting those of Mr. Dean, and directing me to put my Prizes into the hands of Messrs. Gardoqui & Sons, and the principal Merchants at Corunna & Cadiz.—See the Commissioners Letters to Me dated 19th April, 1778

6th. What Mr. Walker here states is by no means the fact.—No such transaction took place, nor was any change made at Saint Antonio. I sailed from thence under my old Papers, in January 1778, and arrived soon after at Bilboa, where I was obliged to change my Articles, as I could not obtain a Crew to sail under the old ones, or to engage for any term beyond a Cruize, but those Articles (unless in this particular), differed very little from the old ones, as the Crew engaged to be govern'd by the regulations made for Seamen in the Continental Service. At Bilboa I paid the Crew their Wages by order of Mr. Gardoqui, from whom I received money for that purpose, Mr. Hodge at the same time made some settlement with the Crew for their prize money—This the Crew insisted should be done, by what authority Mr. Hodge acted I do not know, but I suppose under that of the American Commissioners. I made no settlement whatever with Mr. Hodge. The Several Officers mentioned by Mr. Walker as having deposed, that "I readily subscribed to private articles put on board by Mr. Hodge" were Dr. Smith (a man of a very troublesome & mutinous disposition) his servant boy and one Marine Officer.

7th. The Revenge did take a number of Prizes, all of which I put into the hands of the Principal Merchants of Bilboa, Corunna & Cadiz, and not "into the hands of Mr. Hodge," as Mr. Walker asserts in his report. This will fully appear by the Letters of those Agents to the American Commissioners.

8th. I always acted under the orders of the Commissioners, and none other. I understood (merely by hearsay) that money was advanced by private persons, but did not know the terms of such advance, and I never received the smallest shadow of orders from any private person or persons whatever.

9th. I know nothing of the first part of this Article of report. The two little expeditions, as they are called, I will know were made under the immediate orders of Dr. Franklin & Mr. Dean, the then Commissioners in France, and I never received a Letter from Mr. Ross, much less instructions from him and Mr. Hodge.

10th. This assertion I know nothing of.

11th. Under such Articles as were signed at Bilboa the Revenge sailed to Martinique, yet this did not render her less a public vessell.—Mr. Bingham, the American Agent there, disposed of her as such. See Mr. Binghams Letters.

12. This Article of report needs no reply.

13th. When the revenge came into the Port of Philada.

the Navy Board took the direction of her, and under the orders & direction of that Board she was sold. As to the claims of Mr. Hodge & Mr. Nesbitt I am ignorant of them, but suppose the American Commissioners Letters will explain their foundations.

14 Doctor Franklin as well as Mr. Dean well knew the purpose for which the Lugger Surprize & the Cutter Revenge were bought; and so far was it from the American Commissioners refusing to have any concrn with them, that it was by *their and their Agents* express orders I was uniformly and at all times governed, and into their and their Agents hands the Proceeds of the Prizes went. See the orders of Mr. Secy. Carmichal & others. The last paragraph in this Article of Mr. Walkers report does not merit any other reply than that if any such transaction ever took place I am totally ignorant of it.—

15 This Article of report I know nothing of

16 The American Commissioners Letters[1] and orders to me and to the different Agents will plainly shew she was always considered as a public vessell. See the American Commissioners Letter to me Dated 19th April 1778

Arthur Lee Esqr.   do to Legoneire & Co
                        Novemb 21st 1777
   Ditto. . . . Do. to me . . . .
                     April 26th 1778
   Ditto. . . . Do. do. . . . .
                   Jany 16th. 1778

[1] Not found.

This last letter was laid before the Navy Board in Philadelphia, but it seems cannot now be found.—

17 I admit that the command I was engaged in was intricate in its nature, but I must observe that I did all in my power to prevent any obscurity in the business, so far as related to myself & the Commissioners, under whose authority I acted, and at as early a period as I possibly could laid my claim before the Navy Board in Philadelphia. I know not what Mr. Walker calls sufficient evidence to prove or Justify the idea of the Vessels being private property—for my own part I know of no such evidence existing, nor did I ever consider myself under the direction of any private person or persons.—

18 The Officers alluded to by Mr. Walker were Doctor Smith, the Master at Arms, & the Steward.—If these men come under the description of Officers of the Vessell their testimony might carry some weight, but their assertions are altogether groundless.—Any Gentleman acquainted with Naval transactions must know that men who fill these capacities on board a Vessell of War is altogether deprived of the necessary information to substantiate an assertion of this nature. —The Idea of my dismission and the Command being given to another is distitute of the smallest shadow of truth. It must appear that I did not receive my instructions from Mr. Hodge, but from Mr. Carmichael, Secretary to the American Commissioners at Paris, which will fully appear by refering to that

Gentlemans Letter to me Dated Dunkirk July 15th. 1777.—[1]

19th. Mr. Carmichael came down to Dunkirk for the express purpose of giving me my instructions, but such was the delicacy of our then situation, that great caution and secrecy was necessary to be observed, and the Idea of my receiving instructions from Mr. Hodge is utterly void of any foundation or truth. I believe it will be found that none of the Seamen, who are charged with monies paid them, have pretended to deny the receipt thereof at the times they stand charged therewith. The men who are said in the report to have sworn that they had not received any wages must have been those seamen who were taken in prizes.—If the Navy Board have paid any other they must have paid them to their own prejudice or that of the United States.—

20th. I am very confident (and hope it will not be doubted by any) that I am Justly entitled to all my pay, and a full & compleat reimbursment of all monies advanced on account of these vessels—I also think myself entitled to two twentieths of all prizes sent into Port agreeably to an express Resolve of Congress. The information I have received of the Wl amount of Prizes was from the different agents who received & sold such prizes, and not from Mr. Hodge, as Mr. Walker supposes—I know not how the inference is drawn that Mr Hodge was possessed of the amount of those Sales, but I believe that on inquiry it will be

[1] See p. 64.

found that the Agents have furnished the American Commissioners with particular statements of the Sales of all the Prizes.—I must further observe that the amounts have not been exactly charged in the accounts I have heretofore laid before the late board of Treasury, but as nearly so as I was able from the information I was then possessed of.

21st.   This was sacredly promised to me by the American Commissioners at Paris, which I can prove by living Testimony, when called on.   However extraordinary it may appear to Mr. Walker, it is not unprecedented for Foreign Courts to give up prizes, for Political motives, and to pay the Captors the amount of such prizes.   This has been practised in one or more instances by the Court of France during the time of the American Revolution.

22nd.   This assertion is fully obviated by the Letters of the American Commissioners to me dated the 19 April 1778, wherein they direct me to put the prizes into the hands of Messrs Gardoqui & Sons, of Bilboa, and the principal Merchants of Corunna & Cadiz, which I did & I believe it can be well attested that Messrs. Lagoneire & Co were of this description— Indeed they were the only merchantile House that would make any advances on my arrival at Corunna, and it will be found by the Commissioners Letters to those Gentlemen that they by no means disapproved of their agency, but gave them instructions for the application of proceeds of the prize money.   I never received any instructions on this subject, either from Mr. Hodge or Mr. Conyngham, and I am utterly at a loss to conceive how such Idea could have originated with Mr. Walker, as I am confident nothing can appear to Justify such an assertion.

[EBENEZER GILBERT TO TIMOTHY PICKERING[1]]

Middletown June 10th 1828.

Timothy Pickering Esqr.
Salem.
Hon. Sir,
I take the liberty of addressing you this letter, inviting you to favour me with such information as your situation will permit, while you were one of the Navy Board, at Philadelphia, in the year 1778 & 9, respecting the continental, armed Cutter, Revenge, Gustavus Conyngham Esqr. commander, of 18 guns, who arrived at or near Philadelphia, in the year 1779 from a cruise in the European & Westindia Seas. This Vessel was purchased by order of our Minister, in france; there armed, and the command given to Gustavus Conyngham, by our minister, who was furnished with Blank Commissions by Congress, at the beginning, of our revolutionary war. The command of this Vessel, was given to Gustavus Conyngham, after he had captured the Falmouth Packet, the first British Commissioned Vessel,

[1] Pickering MSS. in the Massachusetts Historical Society, Vol. XXXII, p. 378.

that surrendered to the Flag, of the United States. I am particularly interested to substantiate her character, as a Vessel, belonging to Congress, and it is from you, as one of the Gentlemen of the Navy Board, at that period, that I can call upon; the other gentlemen of that department, I have no knowledge of, and suppose them dead.

Mr. Matthew Lawler, of Philadelphia, who was first lieutenant, commanding on board the Cutter Revenge, referred me to you for information that may be necessary to substantiate her character as a continental Vessel. Mr. Lawler, and myself are probably, the only surviving officers that belonged to her. I was surgeon on board of her in the years 1778 & 9, and hold my certificate of the same, from Gustavus Conyngham, commr., who told me that Congress would reward me for my services, but for which I never called, being independent in my circumstances; but ruinous losses having overtaken me, now in an advanced age, compensation for services in our revolutionary war would be most acceptable, and all that is necessary for that purpose, is to satisfy our government that she was a Vessel belonging to Congress. The Public papers of that Period being partly destroyed by fire, I must solicit your kind office, on this subject, so far as your recollection will authorise you in establishing the character of the Vessel.

I have been thus particular in my communication of the subject, as it may tend to freshen the memory on transactions of fifty years past. The name of Conyngham in our little navy, at the commencement of our revolutionary war was very conspicuous.

Any expense or trouble that my request may occasion you, will be acknowledged with gratitude.

I have the honour to be, Sir

Your mst. Obdt. Servt.

EBENEZER GILBERT.

[Addressed,]
>   Honble. Timothy Pickeringe, Salem, Masstts. per mail. [The postmark stamp is] Middletown Conn June 13.

[Memorandum, in Pickering's hand,]
>   Ebenr. Gilbert, Middletown June 10. 1828 recd. 16th. answd. same day.
>   Answer. I was a member of the Continental *Board of War* & not of the Navy Board, & know nothing of the subject of the inquiry.

INDEX

Adams, John, United States Commissioner to France, 8, 195

Admiral Barrington, privateer, Capture of, table facing 152, 154

Admiralty, Lords of, asked for protection to British commerce, 55

Aguirre, François, & Company, Merchants at Nantes, 132

Allen, Richard, Escape of, 95; Purchases the Greyhound, 56, 57, 66, 72, 73, 75, 84, 90; Reported confined, 83, 93; See also Greyhound, cutter.

Alliance, Continental frigate, Cruise of Conyngham in, 11, 192

Amelot, M., Minister of the Household to Louis XVI, 109, 110

Amphitrite, ship, 22

Amsterdam, Holland, Arrival of Conyngham at, 190, 193; Continental frigate building at, 35; Visit of agent to, 159

Anderson, Pridman, 79

Annual Register, London, extract from, 117

Anville, Comtesse d', 15

Aranda, Count of, 147, 148

Ardent, H. M. S., Capture of, by the French, 172

Arms, from Martinique, 154, 155; From Holland, 159

Arnold, Jonathan, 169, 171

Ash, James, 177

Ashley, James, 79

Audiben, George, Merchant at Marseilles, 126

Audiben, Jos., Merchant at Marseilles, 126

Bache, Richard, 178

Baggot, Captain, 69

Bailey, Benjamin, Prize master of the Northampton, 78, 79, 81, table facing 152

Bancroft, Dr. Edward, an Englishman in the service of the Commissioners, 61

Barbadoes, W. I., table facing 152, 154

Barclay, John, 177

Barclay, Thomas, 177

Bastille, the, Imprisonment of William Hodge in, 3, 83, 88, 90, 91, 94, 95, 96, 98, 105, 144

Beach, Captain, 37, 119

Beach, John, 168

Bean, Captain, 168, 169

Beasly, Stephen, 178

Beatty, John, Colonel, Continental Army, and Commissary-General of Prisoners, 174, 175, 184

Beaumarchais, Caron de, 58, 105

Bell, Captain, 42

Bell, Thomas, 178

Benezet, John, 178

Bergen, Norway, 84

Betbeder, Antoine, Merchant at Saint Sebastien, 132

Betsey, Brig, recaptured by the British, 128, table facing 152

[227]